Other Books by JAMES HASKINS

Diary of a Harlem Schoolteacher
Resistance: Profiles in Nonviolence
Revolutionaries: Agents of Change
The War and the Protest: Vietnam
Profiles in Black Power
A Piece of the Power: Four Black Mayors
From Lew Alcindor to Kareem Abdul-Jabbar
Black Manifesto for Education (Editor)
Religions
The Psychology of Black Language (with Hugh F. Butts, M.D.)
Jokes from Black Folks
Pinckney Benton Stewart Pinchback
Ralph Bunche: A Most Reluctant Hero
Adam Clayton Powell: Portrait of a Marching Black
Witchcraft, Mysticism and Magic in the Black World
Street Gangs: Yesterday and Today
Babe Ruth and Hank Aaron: The Home Run Kings
Snow Sculpture and Ice Carving: The Art of Creating Transient Forms
The Consumer Movement
The Picture Life of Malcolm X
Fighting Shirley Chisholm
The Creoles of Color of New Orleans
Dr. J.: A Biography of Julius Erving
Your Rights: Past and Present
The Story of Stevie Wonder
A New Kind of Joy: The Story of the Special Olympics
Pelé: A Biography
Teenage Alcoholism
Always Movin' On: A Biography of Langston Hughes
The Long Struggle: The Story of American Labor

He was a strange mixture of altruism and egotism, of dreams and action; a servant and a leader. There will never be another like him. (UNITED PRESS INTERNATIONAL)

The Life and Death of Martin Luther King, Jr.

James Haskins

Illustrated with photographs

Lothrop, Lee & Shepard Co.
A Division of William Morrow & Co., Inc. · New York

    4 5 6 7 8 9 10
Library of Congress Cataloging in Publication Data
Haskins, James (date)
    The Life and death of Martin Luther King, Jr.
    SUMMARY: A biography of a man who dedicated his life to the
cause of civil rights, which also reexamines unanswered questions con-
cerning his assassination.
    1. King, Martin Luther—Juvenile literature. 2. King, Martin Luther—
Assassination—Juvenile literature. 3. Afro-Americans—Civil rights— Ju-
venile literature. 4. Afro-Americans—Biography—Juvenile literature.
[1. King, Martin Luther. 2. Afro-Americans—Biography. 3. Civil rights]
I. Title.
E185.97.K5H33   323.4′092′4 [B]   77-3157
ISBN 0-688-41802-3   ISBN 0-688-51802-8 lib. bdg.

Acknowledgments

I am grateful to Mary Ellen Arrington, who typed the manuscript drafts, to Susan Baron for her help with the research and, as always, to Kathy.

Contents

Foreword

Who was Martin Luther King, Jr.? Many of the readers of this book are too young to remember him—what he looked like or the sound of his voice. Yet, the assassination of Martin Luther King, Jr., was one of the greatest tragedies of recent times.

Who is James Earl Ray? Periodically we hear of this imprisoned man, but few of the readers of this book are aware that he is the subject of one of the most controversial mysteries of this century.

This is the story of the tragedy and the mystery surrounding it—of the man who was killed and the man who is accused of the killing, of why the man was killed and why there are many who feel that the case is still open.

Part 1
The Life of
Martin Luther King, Jr.

Chapter 1
Early Years

Atlanta, Georgia, is a large sprawling city at the foot of the Blue Ridge Mountains. Today it is a heavily industrial and cosmopolitan center, known as the unofficial capital of the South, and it is one of the best southern cities for blacks to live in. But back in the late 1920's, before World War II and the growth of industrialization, Atlanta was highly segregated, and for the mass of its black population it wasn't a much better place to live than any other area of the Jim Crow South.

There was a small middle-class black population in Atlanta that avoided some of the more grinding circumstances of black southern life. They were teachers, ministers, doctors. Proud and dignified, they instilled these feelings in their children and promoted education as the means to achieve success. So long as they did not have to go downtown, where they were insulted on the streets and expected to shop in the back of the store and denied the privilege of drinking at soda fountains or eating at lunch counters, they were able to live in comparative dignity in their quiet, well-kept neighborhoods.

One such neighborhood was located in the vicinity of Auburn Avenue in Atlanta, up the hill from a poor black ghetto area. Here the Reverend Martin Luther King, Sr., and his wife Alberta lived in a two-story gingerbread-style house not far from Ebenezer Baptist Church where the Reverend King was pastor. They were highly regarded in the black community, as the families of ministers traditionally were, and their roots were deep within it. Reverend King's father-in-law, Alfred Daniel Williams, had been pastor at Ebenezer Baptist Church for thirty-seven years before him. Mrs. King was a schoolteacher, another profession respected among blacks and which blacks were allowed to pursue. Their children would have many advantages the children of poor black Atlantans did not have.

Christine was their first child. A year later their first son was born on January 15, 1929. He was christened Michael, but shortly thereafter it was decided that he should be named after his father and he was renamed Martin Luther King, Jr. Two years later Martin and Christine had a younger brother, Alfred Daniel, who very soon was called simply "A.D."

The King children had happy, secure first years. Their parents were strict but loving; they emphasized pride and dignity and learning. The house on Auburn Avenue was filled with books. The Reverend King considered his books among his most prized possessions, and well he might have, for he had worked hard to acquire the knowledge that was in them. Born on a farm about twenty miles outside of Atlanta, he had come to the city at the age of fifteen and worked in the freight yards by day while going to school at night. Because of his need to work and the intermittent education he had received on the farm, it took him eleven years to finish high school. He then enrolled in Atlanta's black Morehouse College and five years later he was ordained as a Baptist minister. He had worked hard to get where he was, and he was proud of what he had achieved. He believed he was as good as any other man, black or white, and so he refused to grin and shuffle in the presence of whites, or to keep his head bowed when walking past them to avoid being accused of looking where he shouldn't. In the South in those days such a man was called an "uppity nigger," one who did not know his proper place. Traditionally, uppity niggers did not live long in the South—they were lynched, or their homes were burned down, or they were arrested and jailed. Mrs. King lived in fear that her husband's pride would get him into trouble, but the Reverend King would remind her that one should never fear to do what was right.

Martin, Jr., could not have had a better example of dignity than his father. From his earliest memory, his father's simple statement impressed itself on him. "You are as good as anybody else," the Reverend King would say, and he would look at his son in such a piercing manner that the words would bore into young Martin's brain. He knew them by heart long before he knew what they meant, and he saw his father put those words into action before he understood fully that they referred primarily to the fact that the Kings were black and that being black was a liability in American, particularly southern American, society.

Often when the Reverend King went to downtown Atlanta, he would take one of his children with him. It was necessary for them to learn that there was a world outside their secure neighborhood on Auburn Avenue—a harsh, cruel, segregated world—and it was important that they experience that world in the company of a man whom they trusted and who refused to submit to the indignities whites tried to foist on blacks. When the Reverend King went to downtown Atlanta, he drove his own car, which was out of the ordinary because most black Atlantans rode the city buses. The sight of a black driving a car in the downtown section often signaled "uppity" to white Atlanta policemen, who would stop the driver on some pretext or other. Martin was with his father once when this happened. "Listen boy— " the policeman began. The Reverend King interrupted him. "That," he said, pointing to his small son, "is a boy. I am a man."

In those days, wherever a store's facilities allowed, stores were divided into sections for whites and blacks. Blacks were supposed to shop in the back of the store, whites in the front. The Reverend King would not abide by that custom. Martin was with his father in a downtown shoe store once, in the front section, when a clerk politely reminded the older man that blacks were served in the back. The Reverend King pointed out that the benches in the back were no more comfortable than those in front, and since the shoes were the same he had no intention of moving. If the clerk insisted, he and his son would take their business elsewhere.

These were important lessons for young Martin, but a small child's first personal experience with racial discrimination is something for which he or she can never be prepared. Martin's own experience came when he was about seven. In southern towns and cities, blacks were residentially segregated, but not in large enclaves as in the North. Black sections were interspersed with white sections, and when they were very young the children of both races played freely together. In the white southern mind, small black children were not a bad influence on their own children; it was only after they reached the age when they began to be aware of racial and social differences that suddenly the children of the races had to be separated. Naturally, it was the southern white adults who determined this change in attitude. As the song says, "You've got to be taught to hate and fear." Martin and his small white friend played together, rode their bicycles together, were welcome in each other's homes until the day when his friend's mother informed Martin in a hesitant voice that perhaps he had better not come around there anymore. That was it, the end of a friendship. Martin was not angry—he didn't understand the whole thing enough to be angry. But he realized that it had to do with race: that it was because his skin color was different from that of his friend.

At last it was time for his parents to explain to him what being black meant in America, what it would mean to him for the rest of his life. In simple terms they told him about slavery and about how, through lack of education and opportunity, many black people were still forced to live in poverty and despair. They explained to him about segregation and about how whites expected blacks to act inferior. His mother, especially, warned him against acting "uppity," but she echoed his father's pronouncement, "You are just as good as anybody else." Martin was too young to understand it all, but he was curious. He wanted to find out more about black people and white people, especially about black people. He began to take books out of the library—books about Africa and slavery and great black Americans.

Martin had learned to read at a very young age. All the King children were ready for school before they were old enough to go, for their mother tutored them, anxious for them to get started on their education quickly. Martin learned especially fast, so Mrs. King decided to try to get him into the first grade early. Right after his fifth birthday, in January, she took him to the black school in the neighborhood and enrolled him, telling the teacher that he was six. Everything went smoothly until April when, for some reason, little Martin decided to tell his classmates about his birthday party. "There were five candles on the cake," he said. He was dismissed from school immediately and his mother was told not to bring him back until he was really six. The next year he legally entered first grade, but by then he was so advanced compared to the rest of his class that he was soon transferred to the second grade, where he would have been if the teacher had not found out he was under-age the year before!

Martin quickly absorbed the information he was taught in school and yearned for more. He read his father's library books; he took out books from the library, but sometimes he was not finished reading and rereading them when they were due, so he began to buy books. He had spending money. When he had started asking his parents to buy him things, his father had seen the opportunity to teach his son another lesson in life: you work for what you get. The Reverend King arranged for Martin to have a paper route delivering the *Atlanta Journal*, and with the money he earned Martin bought his books.

He was an intense, quiet boy, almost completely the opposite of his younger brother. A.D. was happy-go-lucky, uninterested in school and a reader of books only when he had to be. His parents' admonitions that he must study in order to get ahead made little impression on him, and yet he was so likable that they found it hard to be stern. Martin, on the other hand, was nearly a perfect son. In fact, he seemed almost too conscientious. One time when their parents were out of the house, A.D. slid down the stair banister and collided so sharply with their grandmother that he knocked her unconscious. Martin, blaming himself for not watching his younger brother more carefully, tried to kill himself by jumping out of an upstairs window.

Serious though he was, Martin also had a keen sense of humor and a love of fun. He was not an abnormal child; he had friends and he enjoyed playing sports, although he was not nearly so good at them as A.D. was. But his intensive quest for knowledge, and also his awareness that he was the brightest in his class, did separate him from others his age. When he was eleven he was enrolled in a special school for exceptionally bright children, where at last learning became a challenge; but the school closed two years later, and Martin was placed in the black high school in his neighborhood. Now he was three grades ahead of other students his age.

By the time he was in high school, Martin had had considerable experience with discrimination and segregation. He had been downtown alone and had felt the various indignities of being ignored, of being passed over in favor of a white customer even though it was his turn in line, of being thirsty and unable to drink from "white" fountains. He could be minding his own business and still be the object of nasty remarks, or he could look up and realize some white person was staring at him suspiciously, just waiting for him to make a wrong move. It all seemed so unfair, and more than that, being black in Atlanta was just plain inconvenient. If you were thirsty, you had to search for a "colored" water fountain, and there never seemed to be a "colored" restroom around, although there were plenty for whites. The arrangement on the city's buses was perhaps the most ludicrous of all. When the bus stopped, you had to enter by the front door, pay your fare, then turn around and push past the other people getting on, go down the steps and around to the door at the back of the bus, the door blacks were supposed to use. It seemed to Martin that if white people were so set on keeping blacks in the back of the bus, they could at least put a fare box by the back door. But running from one door to the other was another indignity that seemed to be imposed on blacks out of sheer spite. What's more, even though they paid the same fare as whites, blacks were expected to give up their seats to whites. Because more blacks than whites used the buses, a larger block of seats was designated for them. But if the white section was filled up, the blacks were expected to give up their seats and stand. Once when Martin was a junior in high school, he and some teachers and fellow students were returning by bus from a debating match at a high school in another town. Martin had not won any prizes and was in a bad mood because of it. The bus stopped at villages along the way, and as more white people got on, the white section of the bus became filled. The driver ordered the blacks in the seats nearest the front to go to the back. Other blacks around Martin did so. Martin remained where he was. It was bad enough not to have won any prizes in the debating match—now this!

The bus driver threatened to call the police if Martin did not move. This warning frightened Martin's teacher, who came forward and softly asked him to move for her sake. Reluctantly Martin got up and went to the back, where he held onto a strap for the remainder of the ride. Going through the adolescent and teen-age years is hard for any young person, but it is doubly hard to develop a sense of self-worth when one is black and living in circumstances of absolute segregation. For Martin, the answer seemed to lie in excelling. He would be better than whites at everything he could be: he had the ability, at least when it came to study and books.

Martin was only fifteen years old when he was accepted as a freshman at Morehouse College, where the emphasis was on preparation for the ministry. The family just assumed that Martin would follow in his father's footsteps, become co-pastor of Ebenezer Baptist Church and eventually assume full pastorship of the congregation. But Martin was not at all sure he wanted to be a minister. He wanted to be something more—a college professor, perhaps, or maybe a lawyer.

He had trouble with his studies that first year. Philosophy was a subject that he was really too young to understand, and if he found it hard to comprehend what he read in his textbooks, it was twice as difficult for him to write papers about what he had read. He continued to read avidly, but on subjects in which he was interested. When it came to studying for his college courses, he procrastinated, went to movies instead, dated girls. He was very much interested in girls. That was one disadvantage to choosing a career in the ministry: one could not have an active social life. Strict Baptists frowned on dances, movies, dating many girls instead of "courting" one.

By his second year at Morehouse, Martin had matured enough to begin to understand the concepts of philosophy, and he became deeply interested in the writings of several religious philosophers. But he had not changed his mind about the ministry; if anything, he was more firmly against entering the profession. He realized that black religion was very different from the types of religion about which he was studying.

The church was the center of black Atlantans' lives; there were far more churches than any other institutions in the black community. It was the only place where they could feel secure, for they believed God cared about them and loved them. Their lives might be hard and demeaning, but if they trusted in the Lord they would be rewarded in heaven. They were happy in church; they were safe in church; in church they could give vent to the emotions they could not show as they worked at low-paying, backbreaking jobs all week. It had been that way since slavery times, and over the decades black religion had evolved into a highly emotional religion—one without much intellectual substance, in Martin's opinion. The poorer the church, the louder the shouting of "Hallelujahs" and "Amens," but even his father's black middle-class church was not lacking in emotionalism. The Reverend King's sermons were filled with exhortations to his parishioners to love God and be patient with the burdens placed upon them during earthly life, for it was just a prelude to heaven, where everyone was equal, the reward for patience. Martin just could not see himself delivering such sermons. He considered going into medicine.

Martin was aware that his family, especially his father, hoped fervently that he would become a minister. At Morehouse one of his professors, Dr. Benjamin Mays, also took an interest in him, believing that his young student had the makings of a fine minister. Martin respected both men, but he had a stubborn streak in him, and the more they encouraged him to consider a career in the ministry, the more he resisted their advice. Rebelling not only against them but against his own judgment and capacities, he became a quarterback on the Morehouse football team. In itself, being a member of the football team was perfectly acceptable, but Martin was not exactly the football type. He was short—only about five feet, seven inches; even A.D. was taller than he was. He was light in weight, and he was not particularly strong. Nor was he especially inclined to athletics other than of the sandlot variety. But he applied himself to football practice as he did to his reading, and somehow he made the team, although he never got to play much. Perhaps for him, making the team was enough; he had set out to prove he could make it and he had. But deep down he realized he would never be a good football player, that he had limitations to which he had to adjust.

The summer after his sophomore year, Martin and some fellow students went north to work in the tobacco fields in Connecticut. Work was plentiful and the pay was better than what they could earn in Georgia; and the young men were understandably curious about the North which, they had heard, was far more racially liberal than the South. Viewed from the surrounding hills, the Connecticut Valley in the summer seemed dotted with lakes. On closer inspection, the lakes proved to be huge, square tents of white gauzelike material covering the shade tobacco which, after being harvested and dried, was used as the outside wrappers for cigars. It was *the* summer industry in the area, and it attracted migrant laborers as well as students from all over the country.

Early in the summer, Martin and his friends helped to "string" the young plants, carefully tying twine to their tender stems and running it up to the nets to assure that the plants would grow tall and straight. It was hot, tiring work, and it took some days before they were able to get over their lameness from bending and stretching, bending and stretching. As the plants matured, their task was to work along the rows, picking the largest leaves and piling them carefully into large canvas containers, which they loaded onto trucks bound for the huge wooden sheds. In the sheds, women and girls sewed the leaves to long, thin wooden lathes, taking care not to damage the leaves. Then men carried the full lathes high up to the sheds' rafters, where the tobacco leaves dried until they were perfect for the wrappings of the finest cigars.

Martin, who had never before worked on a farm, was fascinated by the whole process, although he now understood the value of getting an education. He worked hard in the hot and humid Connecticut summer. Inching along the rows on the seat of his pants, he got dirtier then he had ever imagined he could, and before he got used to it the sticky sap from the tobacco leaves caused him to contract an ailment common among new workers, "tobacco rash." At the end of the day, the sweat and the sticky brown sap congealed in the pores of his skin, and a shower seemed like the ultimate luxury.

Martin compared his experience to that of black southern farm workers—toiling all day in the hot summer sun, picking cotton or sugar cane rather than tobacco. Yet, he realized the experiences were in many ways not comparable. He worked side by side with white local teen-agers who took jobs in the tobacco fields every summer. There was a casual, friendly atmosphere in the fields. The field or "straw" bosses were all white, but most of them treated all their workers the same. At some point, every field worker got a chance to ride the truck to the sheds, where one could laugh and joke with the women and girls, who were primarily white, and not be considered "uppity" or made to feel uncomfortable. At night or on Sundays, when they did not have to work, Martin and his friends would go to nearby towns, where they were served without question at white restaurants and allowed to sit wherever they wanted in the movie theaters. There were no WHITES ONLY signs on Coke machines or water fountains or over doorways. Not everyone was friendly to them, but no one tried to deny them the right to equal use of public facilities. At the end of the summer, the youths boarded a train back to Georgia. While the train passed through the northern states, they sat in the dining car right next to the whites. But as the train reached the South, they were politely asked to move to the rear of the car, and a shade was pulled down to separate them from the rest, as if the sight of blacks in the car would offend the sensibilities of the white diners. Although he was glad to be going home, Martin's experience in the North had a profound effect on him.

That fall and winter Martin thought a lot about the great difference in racial conditions and relations between North and South. If blacks could be treated similarly to whites up there, at least in public places, he did not see why the same situation could not work in the South. Blacks did not walk with their heads down in the North; neither did southern blacks *have* to in the South. He thought about ways to impress his conclusions on his fellow black southerners and realized, with despair, that the best place to reach them was also the place that was most traditional and unchangeable—the church. He had never been able to explain his misgivings about the church to his father, but he could talk to Dr. Mays, who tried to make him understand that it would be possible to be a southern Baptist minister and still appeal to the intellect, not to speak sermons just to invite loud "Amens." For all its deficiencies, the church, Mays reminded him, was the power center of the black community, the place where the greatest number of blacks could be influenced at one time. By the spring of his senior year, Martin had decided to enter the ministry after all.

When his son told him of his decision, the Reverend King was secretly overjoyed. But to Martin he expressed concern that the youth might not have the qualities necessary for a good minister. He knew the scriptures, certainly, but did he have the power to make those scriptures meaningful to people and to their daily lives? Martin said he thought he did. The Reverend King decided to give his son a chance to prove himself by arranging for him to deliver a sermon in one of the small auditoriums of Ebenezer Baptist Church. Seventeen-year-old Martin immediately went to work on his sermon.

Although only a small group of people were invited to hear Martin's sermon, word spread quickly among the congregation of Ebenezer Baptist Church and among Martin's friends and professors at Morehouse. Those who wanted to hear him far outnumbered the seats in the small church auditorium where he had been scheduled to speak. On the Sunday of his sermon, Martin spoke from the main pulpit of the church, looking very young and very small in his white vestment, more like a choir boy than a preacher. But his voice and his words were mature, those of a young, idealistic, earnest man. It was not a radical sermon —Martin did not have the words to express how he felt, nor would he have used them even if he'd had them. He was, after all, in his father's church. And while his style of delivery was less flamboyant than his father's, it was hardly unemotional. Standing up there at that pulpit, looking out at the people assembled in the huge hall, he found he was capable of far more emotion than he had believed. Suddenly, it was very important for him to reach those people, and he succeeded remarkably for one so young. That night, the Reverend King got down on his knees and thanked God for sending him such a son.

Martin was pleased with himself, but he was not surprised; he had said he could do it and he had. But his success meant a turning point in his life. He must now dedicate himself full-time to God, to studying the scriptures in order to understand and interpret them in the light of modern living. He renounced dating and dances, for these were improper activities for a young man who had felt the call to spread the word of the Lord. Once, he succumbed to temptation and went to a dance. Word soon got back to his father, for the Atlanta black community was a fertile place for gossip and the pious churchgoers were concerned with the moral carriage of a young anointed. The following Sunday the Reverend King summoned his son to the main pulpit of the church and demanded an apology.

Martin obliged, but he would find the lack of social life mandated by the church one of the most difficult conditions of the ministry to abide by.

Martin Luther King, Jr., was ordained as a minister when he was eighteen years old, and shortly thereafter he was named assistant pastor of Ebenezer Baptist Church, although he had not yet finished college. It was automatically expected that once he had graduated from Morehouse he would devote his full time to the work of the church, marry a neighborhood girl with whose parents the Kings had a long-term "understanding," and generally follow in his father's footsteps. Martin had other ideas. He felt he needed more schooling. Over the objections of his family that his father had been through only four years of college and that his maternal grandfather had had little formal education, Martin insisted that he should get a master's degree. By the time he graduated from Morehouse College at the age of nineteen, he had been accepted at Crozer Theological Seminary in Chester, Pennsylvania.

Chapter 2
Preparing for
Life in the Ministry

Crozer Theological Seminary had an excellent reputation. It was small, so its students had considerable individual attention from the highly motivated and concerned faculty; and it demanded stringent requirements for both admission and graduation. These were among the reasons Martin had chosen it. But he had another motive: he felt it was important to get away from the insular, small-town atmosphere of Atlanta's middle-class black community and, especially, away from his father. They had established ideas about who a minister was supposed to be and what his ministry was supposed to be like; they expected him to follow in his father's footsteps, to wait patiently throughout his long apprenticeship until his father retired, and then to be a younger version of the elder Reverend King. Martin wanted more, and he did not feel he could develop as an individual, develop his own philosophy, if he stayed in Atlanta. Crozer provided the geographical distance he needed.

Nestled in the rolling green Pennsylvania hills, Crozer was a haven for Martin, for he was protected there not only from the expectations of family and friends but also from the pressures that dog the footsteps of a southern black. He was one of only six blacks in a student body that numbered one hundred, yet he never felt any racial animosity either from his fellow students or from his professors. In fact, he was elected president of the student body. Total emphasis at Crozer was on study and thinking. The students were serious, sure of their calling. There were no football teams; although the students dated occasionally, and Martin more than most, recreation generally took the form of intense after-class discussions of the thoughts of the philosophers and religious thinkers about whom they were reading. For some students the experience was so mind-expanding that it was almost painful. Not for Martin. He welcomed knowledge and could not get enough of it. Partly, this was because he had such an inquiring mind. But partly, too, he was looking for a way to apply philosophical and religious concepts to the plight of southern black people in a new way, one that would take the emphasis off waiting for rewards in heaven— "pie-in-the-sky" it was sometimes called—and place it on gaining rights and dignity enjoyed by other people during earthly life.

One day he went to Philadelphia, to walk around and perhaps visit some bookstores. While there, he learned that Dr. Mordechai Johnson, the President of Howard University, a black institution in Washington, D.C., was scheduled to give a lecture about his recent trip to India. Interested in hearing the distinguished man and having nothing better to do, Martin decided to attend the lecture.

In a very fundamental way, it changed his life. The primary theme of the lecture was the tremendous social change that had occurred in India as a result of the efforts of a former South African lawyer named Gandhi.

Gandhi had been born in India in 1869 to an upper middle-class family and had been educated in his native country and in England, which ruled India. In 1893, as a lawyer in India, he had traveled to South Africa on what was supposed to be a short visit to handle a case for an Indian merchant; he wound up staying twenty-two years. South Africa was—and still is—a very racially segregated society. On the bottom of the social scale were the native blacks, but Indians and other Orientals were treated nearly as badly by the white colonialists. "For Europeans Only" signs were as plentiful in South Africa as "Whites Only" signs in the American South.

Such segregation was difficult for Gandhi to take; in his own country he was in the upper half of the social scale. He tried to improve the conditions of the Indians in South Africa. He joined the South African army and urged his countrymen to do so, believing that they would gain acceptance by proving their support of South Africa's leaders. It didn't work. The Indian soldiers were killed and maimed in the service of the government, but when they were discharged they were still expected to ride wooden benches in third-class carriages and were denied service in public accommodations "For Europeans Only."

Gandhi's South African experience had a profound effect on him. Though he was an upper-class Indian, he came to consider himself one with the other Indians in South Africa, most of whom were peasants. He shed his suit and donned a simple loincloth; he ate what they ate.

Back in India, he had not thought much about the lower classes in his country, about the degradation and inhumanity to which they were subjected—some were considered so lowly that they were called "untouchables." In South Africa, where all Indians of no matter what social class were treated as badly as the untouchables in India, Gandhi came to understand that a social class system was wrong wherever it occurred.

Gandhi was forty-six years old when he returned to his native country, and he looked at it with new and more experienced eyes. He saw that India was nothing more than a British colony and that it was slowly dying under such bondage. India must gain its independence from Britain, he decided, but this could only be achieved by a united people, one not divided by strong caste lines. He began to hold meetings in which he called for independence from Britain, stressing economic independence as a prerequisite for political independence. He set up programs to teach people to provide for their own everyday needs, and explained that even the upper classes should learn to be self-sufficient. He also explained to them that they were too divided and weak to fight the powerful British, but that they could resist the British through non-cooperation and nonviolent protest. The people who heard him understood his economic arguments, but they did not believe that his ideas of non-cooperation would work. Gandhi had to begin nonviolent protest against the British by himself.

On March 12, 1930, Gandhi began a "salt march" to the sea. The British government had a monopoly on salt, and it was against the law for anyone else to make it. Gandhi announced that he would make salt. He was arrested and jailed. He did not try to defend himself. Against the might

of the British authorities he had only his *satyagraha,* or
"soul force." The incident was well publicized, and it
sparked the imagination of the Indian people. Slowly and
in small numbers they began resisting the laws, boycotting
all British goods, refusing to bow to class customs. They
were beaten but, following the urgings of Gandhi, they
did not fight back, and this put the British authorities in a
quandary. Beating defenseless people was poor public
relations. The world was beginning to pay attention to
what was happening in India. The authorities refrained
from beating the resisters and simply put them in jail, but
within two years the jails were filled to overcrowding—it
was almost a disgrace for an Indian *not* to have been in
jail.

The most important thing was to be nonviolent, not to
fight back. Sometimes protesters forgot this and turned to
violence and bloodshed. When they did, Gandhi would
fast, refusing to eat until the violence ended. Eventually,
those who had chosen to react in violence were persuaded
to stop because of Gandhi's "soul force." Remarkable
changes occurred among the Indian people. Untouchables
traditionally had to use different roads so as not to come
too near people of higher classes. Urged by Gandhi to
defy such customs, members of the untouchables class lay
down in the middle of the main roads in protest; they
were joined by people who were already able to use those
main roads. It took years, seventeen long years, but
through the combined effects of Gandhi's "soul force," the
unity of the Indian people against British rule, and
adverse world opinion, the British at last surrendered
India to the Indians. In 1947 Great Britain granted the
country its independence.

Martin left Dr. Johnson's lecture so excited that he

could hardly speak coherently. He went out and bought all the books he could find about Gandhi and his philosophy of nonviolence. He probably would have found some way to travel to India and speak with the great man, but unfortunately the little man who had earned the title of Mahatma, or "Great Soul," was no longer alive. The unity he had achieved among the Indian people against the British had been tenuous. The bitterness and hatred between India's two religious groups, Hindus and Moslems, re-emerged when independence was gained and anti-Moslem riots broke out in many cities. India was partitioned into a Hindu state (India) and a Moslem state (Pakistan). Mahatma Gandhi had turned his attention to uniting Hindus and Moslems, but on January 30, 1948, he was assassinated by a Hindu fanatic who blamed him for the partition of India.

Martin recognized the differences between his country and Gandhi's, where Indians were by far the majority of the population and the former British colonialists had numbered only a few. In the United States, blacks were only about ten per cent of the population and in some ways they were as divided along class and geographical lines as the Indians. Still, he could not get rid of the feeling that somehow Gandhi's philosophy could be applied to the plight of blacks in the United States. He read about Gandhi as a man with a parched palate drinks water. He learned that Gandhi had been influenced by the writings of Henry David Thoreau, so he restudied the writings of Thoreau, especially his essay "Civil Disobedience." Thoreau was an American, born in Massachusetts in 1817, who thought that he should not have to obey laws and customs that he did not believe in. As a young elementary school teacher in Concord he had gotten into trouble by refusing to strike his pupils when they misbehaved. When the authorities insisted that he strike them, he flogged good students and bad students alike, trying to prove his theory that physical punishment had nothing to do with education. It was the first and last time he resisted any law or custom violently!

Beginning in 1838 he protested certain government taxes, such as church and poll taxes. He was excused from paying church taxes, because actually, given the constitutional separation of church and state, local governments had no business imposing such a tax. But the poll tax was another matter. Thoreau never voted, so he did not see why he had to pay a poll tax. The authorities thought differently. In 1846, he was arrested and jailed for non-payment. He spent only one night in jail. His aunt paid his fine, dressed in a disguise because she knew her nephew would be angry if he found out she had paid it. Two years later, Thoreau wrote "Civil Disobedience," in which he recounted his experience in jail and explained why he felt the individual had a right to resist the government in a passive manner. "I was not born to be forced," he wrote. "I will breathe after my own fashion." Some seventy-five years later, in England, Gandhi would read this essay and be influenced by it; just about one hundred years later, in Pennsylvania, Martin Luther King, Jr., would pore over it, searching for answers to his own questions and clues to the solution of the plight of his own people.

Upon Martin's graduation from Crozer, his family was certain he'd had enough education, and they urged him to come home and take up his duties as assistant pastor of Ebenezer Baptist Church. But Martin wanted a doctoral degree. There was so much more to know, and he wanted to learn it. Actually, the senior Reverend King was pleased with his son's ambition. He himself might have done the same if he had been given the same opportunities in his youth. Though he yearned to have his son with him at home, he expressed his approval of Martin's further education by giving him a brand-new green Chevrolet for the trip to Boston College, where Martin had been accepted in the doctoral program in the philosophy department.

In Boston, Martin and his friend Philip Lenud, who was a divinity student at Tufts College, rented an apartment on Massachusetts Avenue, and it soon became a favorite meeting place for black students from both colleges. They talked for hours about political and academic subjects, and Martin loved nothing better than to take a viewpoint opposite his own and debate it. But despite his love for debating, he did not allow his studies to be affected; he was as determined as ever to excel and to get high marks. Among his favorite philosophers in that period was the German Karl Marx, on whose philosophy socialism and communism are based. Martin could not agree with Marx's belief that there is no God, but he could understand the philosophy that a just social order can be gained only if economic wealth is redistributed. Gandhi had begun his movement for independence from Britain by emphasizing economic self-sufficiency, and Martin could look back home to Atlanta and realize that the situation of blacks there would be much better if blacks were allowed to participate more equally in the economic life of the city.

Meanwhile, Martin was enjoying a rather active social life, spurred in part, perhaps, by reminders from home that he was expected to marry the girl with whom he had grown up. It was just one more aspect of the tidy, well-ordered life to which he was supposed to return, and he was determined to explore other possibilities before he did so. But he did not feel particularly comfortable with northern girls, and around Christmas 1951 he began asking his friends if they knew any girls from "down home." Within a short time he was given the telephone number of Coretta Scott.

Coretta Scott was in Boston studying performing arts at the New England Conservatory of Music. Born and raised in Marion, Alabama, she'd had more first-hand experience of southern racism than had Martin. Her father was an "uppity nigger" who through hard work had built a fine home for his family; it had been burned down. He had then built up a successful sawmill business, but when he had turned down an offer from a white man to buy it, it too had been burned. Marion was a rural community, and the black school Coretta had attended was three miles away. She had bitter memories of the white children's school bus careening by on a rainy morning, splashing mud on her freshly starched dress, the children leaning out the windows and shouting "Nigger!" Like Martin, she had decided to be better than whites at whatever she could be, and she was determined to have a career as a concert singer.

Martin fell in love with her immediately. She was a serious, ambitious young woman, far more intelligent than he expected. He had enjoyed the company of other girls, had even thought he loved some of them, but Coretta Scott was the first one he really respected. Over the following months they dated constantly, and Cora realized that she, too, was in love. But she had grave misgivings about their relationship. She liked living in the North and did not want to return to the degrading conditions under which blacks lived in the South. Martin, on the other hand, fully intended to return to the South, where he hoped to inspire his fellow blacks to assume the dignity denied them by whites. He expected his wife to be a proper minister's wife, while Coretta wanted to be her own woman. Marrying Martin would mean giving up the career about which she had dreamed for so long. In the summer of 1952 she consented to visit Martin and his family in Atlanta, and her experience there only confirmed her worst fears. If she and Martin married and went to live in Atlanta, their lives would not be their own; they would be dominated by the Reverend King.

Coretta Scott hoped for a compromise. She wouldn't mind being the wife of a Baptist minister if they remained in the North. Parishioners up there were more liberal in their views about proper conduct for a minister's wife. Up there, she could perform on the stage and not be socially ostracized by her husband's church. Whatever happened, however, she would marry Martin, for her heart had over-ruled her head. On June 18, 1953, they were married on her father's lawn in Marion, Alabama, in a ceremony per-formed by the Reverend King.

In the fall they returned to Boston, where Martin went on with his doctoral studies and Coretta continued her work at the New England Conservatory, although she switched her major from performing arts to music. While Martin had not yet completed his doctoral thesis, that fall he began to get job offers. He was invited to become pastor of a church in Boston and one in New York; he was offered a position on the faculty of a northern college, a deanship by another, an administrative post by still another. He rejected all of them. He was determined to return to the South. But by now he was equally determined not to return to the home of his father and Ebenezer Baptist Church. He wanted to have his own church, where he could act independently and not have to function under the wing of another man.

In late fall he received a letter from the elders of the Dexter Avenue Baptist Church in Montgomery, Alabama. The church was without a pastor, and he was invited to be a guest preacher one Sunday when he was in the area. Martin wrote back that he could do so on a Sunday in January. In the interim, he wrote to some friends and acquaintances to inquire about the church and was pleased to learn that its congregation was made up of middle-class professional people. He wanted nothing to do with poor southern churches that were all emotionalism. One cold January Sunday he and Coretta stood across the street and looked at the Dexter Avenue Baptist Church. It was a small red brick structure with white doors and steeple on well-kept grounds on Montgomery's main street. Inside, as they were graciously greeted by the church elders, they noticed the gleaming polished wood of the pews and the stained-glass windows. It was a place where they could feel at home, where they could belong.

Martin's sermon was highly successful. It should have been; he'd worked hours on it. He left Montgomery without asking for the pastorship of the church, but soon after he was back in Boston the letter of invitation arrived. Martin and Coretta talked about the matter for some time before he responded. She was still against leaving the North, but if she had to go South she preferred Montgomery, which was seventy or eighty miles from Marion where her family was, to Atlanta. In the end, they decided on a sort of compromise. Martin would accept the offer of Dexter Avenue Baptist Church, but he would inform them that he and Coretta could not move to Montgomery until September. In the meantime, they would commute between Montgomery and Boston, with stopovers in Atlanta where they could visit his family and he could work on his doctoral thesis, which he still had to submit to earn his degree. It was a trial period that would enable them to get used to their new life gradually. But they both knew the move to Montgomery was inevitable, for Martin had decided Dexter Avenue Baptist Church would be his, and he usually got what he wanted.

In September 1954 Martin and Coretta King moved into the old seven-room white frame parsonage in the middle of Montgomery's black middle-class neighborhood, and while Coretta went to work making it home for them, Martin went to work on his church. It would be his church, even though many of the elders were twice as old as he was. One of the first things he did was to abolish the system of collections during services. His father did not like the idea of passing collection plates around on Sunday, and neither did he. Henceforth, donations were to be made directly to him or to one of the elders. The elders agreed to the change. What they did not agree to was his suggestion that they actively recruit new parishioners from among the poorer blacks in Montgomery. Among these blacks the Dexter Avenue Baptist Church was known as the "rich man's church"; Martin wanted them to feel free to come to it, to have the opportunity to hear his sermons. The church elders, however, would not hear of it, and Martin knew better than to insist on such a radical change when he was still so new to the church. He was amazed, however, at the strong class divisions among the black people of Montgomery.

Compared to Montgomery, Atlanta was downright liberal. The same segregated conditions prevailed, but white attitudes about blacks and their "place" were even more deeply ingrained in Montgomery, and being "uppity" was even more dangerous. When he had first arrived, Martin had been warned by many people not to try to resist or question the prevailing social order. Coretta understood what they meant, for she had grown up under such cir-. cumstances. Martin was troubled by what he saw, particularly by the divisions within the black community that he realized were a result of the extreme racism of Alabama's whites. Sometimes he wished he were more like his brother A.D., who had also become a minister in his own time and in his own fashion. A.D. had remained in Atlanta, where he was comfortable, where he knew what to expect and what was expected of him. Martin wanted to bring about change, and there were times when he wondered if it might not have been easier in the city where he had grown up.

He became friends with another young black pastor in Montgomery, the Reverend Ralph David Abernathy, who told him much about his new home. Abernathy, pastor of the First Baptist Church, had grown up in Montgomery and was accustomed to its racially vicious ways. Together, the two talked about the possibilities for change. About a year earlier, in May 1954, the United States Supreme Court had ruled in the *Brown vs. Topeka Board of Education* case that segregated schools for whites and blacks, even though they were supposedly "separate but equal," were unconstitutional. It was the first break in the solid wall of segregation that had stood across the South since shortly after the Civil War, and those who understood the ramifications of the ruling realized that it could establish a precedent for striking down "separate but equal" provisions in public accommodations as well.

King and Abernathy discussed these possibilities, but they were too realistic to expect the Supreme Court decision to have much effect on the South even in their lifetimes. The southern states would resist any attempts to change the traditional social system, particularly when movement for such change involved the federal government's interfering in affairs they considered the business of the states. The decision inspired a great deal of talk, but no discernible action, and not for another year would the Supreme Court justices realize that the ruling was worthless unless provisions were made whereby it would be obeyed. They then ordered the federal courts to ensure that the ruling be implemented "with all deliberate speed." Just what this meant, of course, was subject to interpretation. "Deliberate speed"—a year? two years? ten years? Federal courts in most southern states preferred a broad interpretation and did nothing. But here and there a courageous federal judge began to order the first tentative steps toward school desegregation.

In response to these attempts to alter the social order in the South, southern white racists became more determined than ever to keep blacks "in their place," and even racial moderates began to support increased suppression of blacks. Racial demonstrations occurred with greater frequency, various White Citizens Councils increased in numerical strength, and the Ku Klux Klan, which had practically died out, revived markedly. Martin Luther King, Jr., was not intimidated by this situation. He was determined to raise the political consciousness of his parishioners no matter what occurred in the larger society. In fact, he had less faith in man's law than he did in moral law. He realized that if the South were forced by government to let down its racial barriers, it would bitterly resent the black man. He preferred a less antagonistic course and believed that if whites could be made to see blacks as helpless, oppressed people and not people to be either feared or hated, then desegregation would be a natural and peaceful result.

In the meantime, his parishioners could do more than they were doing to help their own situation. They could establish community projects to help less fortunate blacks. They could make their presence felt by exercising their right to vote. They could join the National Association for the Advancement of Colored People, whose lawyers had been instrumental in bringing about the *Brown vs. Topeka Board of Education* decision. Beyond such activities, he himself was not sure what could be done to advance the cause of southern blacks. He certainly had no clear-cut plan for achieving social equality.

The seed for such a plan was planted in December 1955. Mrs. Rosa Parks, a seamstress who worked in a downtown Montgomery department store, boarded a bus early on the evening of December 1 and took a seat in the fifth row behind the first four "whites only" rows. She was tired and as she gazed out the window she did not notice that with each stop the bus was rapidly filling with people and that all the seats were taken. The driver looked back to see that a few whites were standing. He told the blacks who were sitting immediately behind the white section to get up. Mrs. Parks remained in her seat. The driver pointed to Mrs. Parks and ordered her to give up her seat. "No," she said. She was tired, she had worked all day, and she refused to give up her seat to a white man who had paid the same fare as she. The driver looked at the thin, bespectacled woman, her hair pulled back in a neat bun, her white-gloved hands folded in her lap, and decided *he* wasn't going to be cast in a bad guy role. He went to look for a policeman. The officer arrested Mrs. Parks and took her to the station house where he booked her for violating a Montgomery city ordinance concerning racial accommodation on public transportation. He would later regret charging her with that particular misdemeanor.

Incidents like this were not infrequent, but in recent years blacks arrested for refusing to give up their seats to whites had been charged under the broad heading "disorderly conduct." It was no secret that the NAACP and individual leaders in the civil rights struggle were looking for test cases to challenge segregation laws. "Disorderly conduct" was a safe charge; violation of a racial accommodation ordinance was not. For several months a black women's group, the Women's Political Council, had been looking for just such a reason to stage a boycott of Montgomery's buses. A stout Pullman porter named E. D. Nixon, one of Montgomery's most outspoken blacks, had also been looking for a way to demonstrate to Montgomery's whites the economic leverage of the city's 48,000 blacks. The city's black activists formed a committee to organize a one-day black boycott of buses, and desiring to have black ministers represented on the committee, they asked Martin to be on it. Martin was reluctant to accept. He had as much work as he could handle as pastor of his church, and in addition he had a brand-new daughter. His and Coretta's first child had been born on October 15, 1955; she was christened Yolanda Denise, but already they were calling her Yoki. Martin felt his first duties were to his church and his family. Yet, this boycott idea excited his imagination. He accepted a place on the committee.

There wasn't much time. The day of the boycott must be soon, and Monday, December 5, was chosen. The committee rushed to get leaflets distributed throughout the black community saying, "Don't ride the bus on Monday, December 5." One fell into the hands of the white *Montgomery Advertiser*, which published it on Sunday, December 4—the best publicity the committee could have hoped for. The committee also contacted black taxi companies and arranged for their cabs to be stationed at strategic points in the black community, to pick up riders and transport groups of riders at reduced fares; they urged car pools and even walking to work as alternatives to riding the buses. Most of the black ministers agreed to devote their Sunday sermons to the boycott.

Martin still had grave misgivings about the boycott. It seemed, in a small way, as bad as the actions of the white racist groups—a negative act, not a positive, Christian one. He worried that it might somehow be immoral. Then, suddenly, it occurred to him that what he and the rest of the committee were planning was right in line with the philosophy of Henry David Thoreau. He remembered a passage from Thoreau's essay "Civil Disobedience": "We can no longer lend our cooperation to an evil system." Non-cooperation was not immoral; in fact non-cooperation with evil was highly moral. All at once he felt energized, eager for the boycott to succeed; he prayed that it would succeed.

Martin and Coretta were awake and up before dawn on Monday morning, December 5. They stationed themselves at one of the front windows, from which vantage point they could see a bus stop on Highland Avenue. The first bus was due at 6 a.m.; no blacks waited at the stop. Martin and Coretta held their breath as the bus approached, and shouted for joy as it passed. The normally crowded bus was empty! Throughout the morning they kept their vigil. On some buses they saw a few white passengers, but no blacks—not one single black! It was, in almost the literal sense of the word, a miracle. All over the city blacks walked, or hitched rides, or shared private cars and taxis. In the entire city of Montgomery, only eight blacks were seen riding on the buses, and since blacks constituted seventy percent of the ridership the buses were virtually empty all day.

That afternoon Mrs. Rosa Parks came to trial. She was fined ten dollars, plus four dollars for court costs. The judge was informed by black attorney Fred D. Gray that the decision would be appealed. Gray and the others behind the boycott were overjoyed that a fine had been imposed, for it kept their case alive, and they were determined to take it all the way to the Supreme Court if necessary. Once they saw how successful the one-day bus boycott had been, they were determined to build on that momentum.

Late Monday afternoon, the black ministers met with Gray, Nixon, and other activist leaders and voted to continue the boycott and to elect a more permanent committee. To his surprise, and to that of many others at the meeting, Martin heard his name put into nomination for president. His was the only name placed in nomination and he was elected unanimously. He accepted immediately; only later did he realize how much additional work the position would entail, and the potential danger in which he was placing himself. The permanent committee was named the Montgomery Improvement Association. A

The Dexter Avenue Baptist Church in Montgomery, Alabama, where Martin Luther King, Jr., assumed his first pastorship was headquarters for the Montgomery bus boycott. (WIDE WORLD PHOTOS)

meeting had been scheduled for that evening at the Holt Street Church. As the president of the new association, Martin would be expected to speak. He did not have time to prepare his speech; he only had time to pray.

Perhaps it was best that he did not have time to write a speech. If he'd had time, he might have spoken from his head more than from his heart, and this was the moment to speak from the heart. They were entering on a frightening adventure whose outcome was unknown. In a very real way, the people in the Holt Street Church that night were putting their homes, their jobs, their very lives on the line. They needed inspiration and they needed hope and they needed to believe they were doing the right thing. Martin Luther King, Jr., speaking from his heart, gave them what they needed:

Preparing for Life in the Ministry • 47

"One of the great glories of democracy is the right to protest for right," he said. "The White Citizens Councils and the Ku Klux Klan are protesting for the perpetuation of injustice in the community. We are protesting for the birth of justice in the community. . . . Their methods lead to violence and lawlessness. But in our protest there will be no cross burnings. No white person will be taken from his home by a hooded Negro mob and brutally murdered. There will be no threats and no intimidation. We will be guided by the highest principles of law and order. Our method will be that of persuasion, not coercion. We will only say to the people: 'Let your conscience be your guide.' Our actions must be guided by the deepest principles of our Christian faith. Love must be our regulating ideal. Once again we must hear the words of Jesus echoing across the centuries: 'Love your enemies; bless them that curse you, and pray for them that despitefully use you.'"

Martin Luther King, Jr., was twenty-six years old, and he had spent eleven of those years reading the works of the world's great philosophers. During his late teens and early twenties, he had in his youthful arrogance wanted to develop an entirely new philosophy, one that could be claimed by no one else in history. He did not understand, or refused to recognize, that just about everything worth thinking has already been thought. But he was beginning to combine, in his own individual way, the ideas of Jesus, Gandhi, and Thoreau. He would later add those of Karl Marx and other philosophers. And through that synthesis of the different and sometimes divergent ideas of those who had gone before him, he was forming a philosophy of his own, one that would one day be called great. At the time, even he did not realize it.

Chapter 3
The Early Civil
Rights Movement

There was no set number of days or weeks for this boy-cott. The Montgomery Improvement Association called for blacks to stay off the buses until three demands had been met. One was guaranteed courteous treatment by bus drivers. The second was the employment of black bus operators on black routes (the bus companies employed no black drivers). And the third was an agreement that passengers would be seated on a first-come, first-served basis, regardless of race. That the arrangement called for blacks sitting from back to front and whites sitting from front to back indicates that Montgomery's black activists were still quite timid in their demands. A decade later they would not feel the need for such compromise.

But by 1965 the racial atmosphere in Montgomery would have changed considerably. In 1955, the civil rights movement was just beginning to move out of the courts and onto the streets, and the danger in those streets was real and ever-present. Blacks were challenging several aspects of life in Montgomery, not the least of which was the economic livelihood of its downtown section. The buses were not operated by the city, but by an outside company, based in Chicago, and thus the city did not suffer financially from the boycott. But the downtown stores, made accessible to blacks by the buses, did.

They were also challenging the laws of Montgomery, such as the public accommodation ordinance under which Rosa Parks had been charged. And finally, they were challenging the traditional social order. Many whites, although they did not realize it, maintained their very identities at the expense of blacks. As long as they had blacks to step on and spit upon, they were "somebodies" in their own eyes; they might work in dull, dead-end jobs, be ill-educated and have little hope for the future, but they could always take heart in the existence of the "lowly nigger." Other whites, those in better economic and social circumstances, simply did not understand what blacks were complaining about. These whites believed they had always been good to the blacks in their employ and did not realize that blacks had the same human feelings as they did. Economics had been the reason for the relegation of blacks to second-class status, and earlier, the agricultural base of the southern economy had depended on slavery. By the 1950's the southern economic base had changed from agriculture to industry and the caste system of the South had become primarily a social one, based on tradition and ignorance. But people's egos are quite as vulnerable as their pocketbooks, and they will defend one just as viciously as the other. This was the situation the Montgomery Improvement Association and its followers faced.

Most blacks stayed off the buses. Of the 17,000 black bus riders, some 14,500 observed the boycott. Immediately, the white community retaliated. White employers told black workers that if they did not ride the buses they would be fired; ninety-five percent of the black workers threatened in this way quit their jobs. City officials threatened to close the black taxi companies, whose licenses contained a ruling that they were not to charge less than forty-five cents per ride (during the boycott, they were charging each passenger ten cents a ride, the same as the bus fare). In response, King and other leaders doubled their efforts to organize car pools and were so successful that the Montgomery White Citizens Council described the pools as working with "military precision," as if there were secret, militaristic forces working behind Montgomery's normally timid, disorganized blacks. When the city formally notified the black taxi companies that their practices during the boycott were illegal, the companies were forced to discontinue their special services. But the story hit the national press wires and donations poured in from across the country. Soon, ten black churches had ten new station wagons to replace the black-owned taxis.

The growing national attention to what was going on in Montgomery only reinforced the determined resistance on the part of racist whites in the city. The mayor joined the White Citizens Council in a public act of defiance. The members of the Montgomery Improvement Association began receiving hundreds of obscene and threatening phone calls. As the MIA's president, Martin received the most, and for the first time he began to consider the possibility of violent death. On Monday January 30, 1956, his house was bombed for the first time.

He was not at home that evening. Coretta was entertaining some women friends while Yoki slept in a bedroom at the back of the house. They heard a crash, then smoke filled the house. One of the women began to scream.

When Martin arrived home, summoned by a brief and frightening telephone call, he found his house filled with people and the street outside jammed with onlookers. Montgomery Mayor W. A. Gayle and Commissioner Clyde Sellers were on the Kings' front porch. They had rushed to the scene of the bombing to assure everyone that they deplored such violence. Now, they were frightened. The crowd of blacks was angry; police stood ready to quell any disturbance. When Martin arrived, both Gayle and Sellers grabbed him and expressed their sympathy. The crowd was not mollified. Someone began to shout the words of "America": "My country 'tis of thee, sweet land of liberty . . ." There was nothing sweet about the voices that took up the song; they were bitter, filled with rage, dangerous.

Having seen for himself that Coretta and Yoki were all right, Martin turned to the most immediate problem. The crowd might lose control at any moment. He made his way to the front of his porch and held up his arms. He spoke to them in reassuring tones. His wife and baby were all right, he told them. He was all right. They must not let their anger hurt the nonviolent cause for which they were working. He quoted Jesus. He spoke of love. Gradually the crowd quieted. Then, Martin Luther King, Jr., channeled the high emotion of the crowd from negative to positive and made his first public utterance about the possibility of his own death: "Remember, if I am stopped, this movement will not stop because God is with this movement. Go

On January 30, 1956, the young Reverend Dr. King stood in front of his bombed home in Montgomery and quieted the angry crowd of blacks gathered outside. Neither Mayor Gayle (in uniform) nor Commissioner Sellers (right) had been able to disperse the crowd before Dr. King's arrival, and from that night on they realized that he was a leader to be reckoned with. (UNITED PRESS INTERNATIONAL)

home with this glowing faith and radiant assurance." Shouting "Amen!" amid tears, the crowd dispersed.

Back in Atlanta, Martin's father decided the time had come to demand that his son leave Montgomery. He had been worried ever since this boycott business had begun. Now, his son's home had been bombed. He didn't care how successful Martin had been in quieting the crowd of blacks outside his house—blacks were not the trouble. But Martin Luther King, Sr., might just as well have saved his breath. Something important had happened on that front

The Early Civil Rights Movement • 53

porch in one of Montgomery's black sections that night. Martin Luther King, Jr., had controlled an angry and vengeful crowd. The Mayor and the Commissioner had witnessed it; the national wire services had reported it; but perhaps most important of all, Martin had done it. The incident only increased his sense that he had been somehow "called," like Moses, to lead his people out of inequality and despair; "called," like Gandhi, to lead the soul force that would change an entire nation.

Unlike Gandhi, however, Martin was not ready to be a martyr. He had never seriously considered fasting, and he certainly was not going to expose himself to a violent death if he could help it. He began to imagine being led away by police in the dead of night and delivered to a lynch mob. He applied at police headquarters for a permit to carry a gun. When asked his reasons, he cited the bombing of his house and the hundreds of threatening telephone calls he had received. The police denied him the permit, and gleefully notified the news media that the "great" advocate of nonviolence had sought to acquire a weapon of violence. The resulting publicity was bad. He could not espouse the philosophy of nonviolence and own a gun, not if he wanted to be a leader in the civil rights cause. He weighed the potential danger to himself and his family against his potential as a real moral leader of his people. He did not reapply for a gun permit; instead, he had floodlights installed around his house and hired a bodyguard.

The bus boycott continued, and white resistance mounted. The White Citizens Council held rallies and distributed leaflets that viciously parodied the Declaration of Independence: "When in the course of human events it becomes necessary to abolish the Negro race, proper methods should be used. Among these are guns, bows and arrows, sling shots and knives. We hold these truths to be self-evident, that all whites are created equal with certain rights, among these are life, liberty and the pursuit of dead niggers . . ." The police sent inquiries all over the country trying to find out whether there were any members of the Montgomery Improvement Association with previous arrest records. Some had them, and these records were well publicized. Blacks who did not observe the boycott were the brunt of white cruelty, for they were black, after all, and thus likely targets. A blind black man was dragged several yards, his foot "accidentally" caught in a bus door; another man was shot after he had paid his fare, been told the bus was too crowded, and demanded it back. Bombings of black homes continued. The more white violence occurred, the greater the coverage of the boycott in the press; and the more press coverage the boycott received, the more national attention and sympathy were aroused. Contributions poured in to the MIA, and the inevitable happened. Whenever power and money are concentrated, especially whenever and wherever they are concentrated suddenly, factional disputes develop. Some members of the MIA were jealous of King and the other leaders, and, given the small-time quality of the Association's accounting procedures, there were legitimate questions about where the money was going. Martin managed to bring about the necessary reconciliations with remarkable success. His argument, and his purpose, were to maintain a united black front during the boycott. If the whites discerned a crack in that front they would exploit it, and the boycott would fail.

The matter of discrimination on Montgomery's buses and of the boycott was before the courts, and had been for a long time. It had gone to the local courts, to the Federal District Courts—long months of filing briefs and delays and appeals. The matter had been brought to the courts in a variety of cases. In one case, the city had charged that the Montgomery Improvement Association was, through its car pool, operating an unlicensed transit system. In another case, more potentially destructive to the boycott, the MIA was indicted for violating a state ordinance against conspiring against private business. But courts are not above the influence of public opinion. King and other Montgomery leaders realized that their chances to win their court cases depended greatly on the success of the boycott. It was becoming harder to maintain the boycott's momentum. By September 1956, blacks had been off the buses for nine months and they were tired of walking and riding in car pools. By November, both whites and blacks were just about at the end of their ropes, and tempers on both sides were short.

On November 13, 1956, Alabama Circuit Court Judge Eugene Carter convened the session that would decide the legality of the car pool. In the midst of the arguments, an AP reporter handed a short piece of teletype paper to Martin Luther King, Jr. He had to read it twice before he could comprehend it. The Supreme Court of the United States had declared segregation on Montgomery's buses unconstitutional. The relief he felt caused him to lose his usual public poise. It was the decision they had all been hoping for, and yet when it came he suddenly felt tired, very tired. Coretta was in the back of the courtroom. Instead of making a triumphant announcement, he went directly to her, and together they went home.

As the leader of the successful Montgomery bus boycott, the Reverend Dr. King was in great demand as a speaker. Many young whites were receptive to his pleas for black equality. (WIDE WORLD PHOTOS)

When the meaning of the Supreme Court decision finally sank in, Martin was jubilant, as were all the blacks in Montgomery. Many of the whites were furious. That night the Ku Klux Klan staged one of its night rides through the black community. Slowly, forty automobiles filled with men in white hoods passed through the streets. Always before, the fearful blacks had turned out their lights and huddled together in terror. This night, they turned on their porch lights or floodlights and waved at what had changed suddenly from a frightening to a rather pathetic sight.

The Early Civil Rights Movement • 57

Martin was afraid the blacks would become too fearless, too cocky. There would be acts of provocation from whites, and he did not want blacks to respond violently. Otherwise, the victory of the boycott would be nullified. The whole country would be watching Montgomery's blacks; how they behaved had crucial meaning to the future of the civil rights movement. Black ministers began to hold classes in nonviolence in their churches; King and his committee went from church to church and to the local high schools and colleges to conduct nonviolence training classes. Chairs would be set up to resemble bus seating arrangements, and people would act out situations that were likely to occur. Some played the roles of whites who made insulting remarks, others the roles of black bus passengers. Over and over, they practiced keeping their self-control, not reacting to insults or pushing. A few days before Christmas 1956, the Supreme Court decree was officially served on the city and blacks went back to the buses prepared, Martin fervently hoped, to withstand whatever cruel or violent treatment they were subjected to.

Bricks were thrown through bus windows . . . black women were slapped . . . black men were beaten; but they did not fight back. A shotgun blast shattered a door in the King home . . . there were scattered bombings. Whites boycotted the buses, but since they represented such a small percentage of the ridership their absence had little impact.

The boycott over, attendance at MIA meetings fell off, and Martin Luther King, Jr., became restless. He did not want momentum for change in the racial structure of the South to end with that one victory. In other parts of the

South, black ministers saw the possibilities for change in their communities, based on Montgomery's precedent. Reverend C. K. Steele of Tallahassee, Florida, issued a call for a conference of southern black ministers for January, 1957, in Atlanta. King and Abernathy decided to attend. A new organization would emerge from that meeting, the Southern Christian Leadership Conference (SCLC), whose purpose was a general one, to urge the federal government to pass civil rights laws and to promote the movement for black equality in the South. Martin would be elected president.

While they were in Atlanta, several blacks' homes in Montgomery, including Abernathy's, were bombed. Immediately, the mayor and the commissioner used the bombings as an excuse to cancel all bus service in the city, stating that buses loaded with blacks were prime targets for bombs. Returning to Montgomery, Martin called a mass meeting to pray for guidance. But he wasn't feeling particularly inspirational. Their victory had been nullified; blacks were walking once more. Up in the pulpit, he broke into tears. "Lord," he shouted, "I hope no one will have to die as a result of this struggle for freedom in Montgomery. Certainly, I don't want to die. But if anyone has to die, let it be me, Lord." The effect was electric. Once again, the blacks were united behind their leader. A few days later, the violence ended. Two white men were arrested for the bombings but were acquitted by an all-white jury. Bus service was reinstituted. The MIA leadership nucleus was transferred to the SCLC, which was still looking for a specific program or activity to sponsor. By May, the organization had that activity, and Martin introduced the idea at a Prayer Pilgrimage in Washington, D.C., sponsored by the

National Association for the Advancement of Colored People, the first mass meeting of civil rights groups and their supporters in the nation's capital. King was to be one of the last speakers, and he worried that by the time his turn came the huge crowd assembled between the Lincoln Memorial and the Mall would be tired and restless. He needn't have worried. Martin Luther King, Jr., had become a new American hero. Publicity for the Montgomery bus boycott had also been publicity for him. He had even appeared on the cover of *Time* Magazine. Many in the crowd that had assembled in the hazy Washington sun that afternoon of May 17, 1957, had come especially to hear him.

"Give us the ballot, and we will no longer plead—we will write the proper laws on the books," he intoned, his deep voice rumbling across the suddenly silent assemblage. "Give us the ballot, and we will fill the legislatures with men of good will." The crowd roared its approval. "Give us the ballot, and we will get the people judges who love mercy. Give us the ballot, and we will quietly, lawfully implement the May 17, 1954, decision of the Supreme Court. Give us the ballot, and we will transform the salient misdeeds of the bloodthirsty mobs into the calculated good deeds of orderly citizens." He was the hit of the day. The crowd would not stop cheering, stomping, clapping. They were ready to follow him. Shortly thereafter, the SCLC announced the inauguration of its Cru-

Known as a troublemaker, Martin Luther King, Jr., was often arrested by southern law enforcement officials on any pretext. Here he is being taken to court for a hearing on an alleged traffic violation. (WIDE WORLD PHOTOS)

sade for Citizenship, a non-violent drive for voter registration of blacks in the South.

That summer, King's self-confidence and his considerable ego were deflated a bit. Raganath Diwakar, a Hindu disciple of Gandhi, flew to Montgomery to speak with the foremost American exponent of nonviolence, a man whose true commitment to Gandhi's principles Diwakar seriously questioned. In the Indian's view, King had not shown a willingness to suffer personally the way Gandhi had. He had never gone on a fast; he wore expensive suits and owned two cars. Every time he had been arrested, he had either been released on his own recognizance or bailed out. Listening to the man, King felt ashamed. He was too much his own man—and too much an American—to do a complete turnabout and become a black Gandhi. But he did realize the truth in Diwakar's advice that he ought to show some sort of personal sacrifice as an example to his followers. He decided that the next time he was arrested he would stay in jail—an action that not only would prove his personal commitment but also would gain publicity for his cause.

Late that summer, the first federal civil rights bill since 1875 was passed. It created a Civil Rights Commission to look into voting irregularities, and authorized the Department of Justice to send out court injunctions to southern states where poll taxes were charged and literacy tests were required. Both these measures had long been used to keep blacks in the South from voting. Poll taxes were usually not large—one or two dollars per year—but still, for some blacks they were prohibitive—and sometimes they were charged retroactively. In other words, if a black had not voted since 1942 and he wanted to register in

1956, he had to pay one or two dollars for each year he had not voted, and fourteen dollars or twenty-eight dollars was indeed prohibitive. Literacy tests theoretically established only whether a prospective voter could read and write, but the definition of literacy was left up to each individual county. Many counties asked blacks questions that hardly anyone could answer, and when they could not respond judged them ineligible to vote because they had failed the literacy test.

The Commission, however, was not given sufficient power to do much about such voter registration irregularities. In fact, the bill itself was very weak—a compromise measure designed to mollify civil rights activists by giving them the false impression that the government supported their cause. Southern legislators were adamantly against federal intervention in the affairs of their states, and the rest of the country was not sufficiently committed to civil rights to bring much pressure on the South.

Back in the South, despite many rallies and inspirational speeches by King and others, the movement to register more black voters could hardly be called a crusade. Something was lacking—commitment, energy, a sense of unity and driving purpose. The fervor that had characterized the Montgomery bus boycott was lacking. King was hard put to explain why.

Late in the summer of 1958, King's first book, *Stride Toward Freedom*, was published, and he went to New York for an autographing session at Blumstein's department store in Harlem. Many Harlem blacks did not think much of his nonviolent philosophy; though most were originally from the South or had southern-born parents, they had been changed by the northern urban experience.

Dr. King and Mrs. Rosa Parks, the woman whose refusal to give up her seat to a white man sparked the Montgomery bus boycott and brought King to national prominence. (UNITED PRESS INTERNATIONAL)

Theirs was not the slow, predominantly rural life-style of southern blacks. The discrimination they suffered as blacks was different and promoted a far more militant attitude toward the civil rights struggle. King was surprised to hear boos from the crowd as he arrived at Blumstein's. In the store, he sat autographing his books for a line of buyers, mostly women. They were friendly, admiring; the atmosphere inside the store was completely different from that outside. He looked up and smiled at a woman who stood by the desk. Yes, he was Dr. King, he said in answer to her question. Suddenly, his smile changed to a grimace of horror. The woman pulled a letter opener out of her pocket and plunged it deep into his chest!

He was rushed to Harlem Hospital, where doctors worked hours performing the delicate operation to remove the blade, which had come so close to his heart that even a cough could have caused massive hemorrhaging and death. After he regained consciousness, practically his first concern was for his would-be assassin. He realized she was deranged and was anxious that charges not be pressed against her. To police and reporters, the woman, Mrs. Izola Curry, charged that King was a communist. In the next breath she said he was trying to convert her from Roman Catholicism. She thought he was head of the NAACP. She was sent to Bellevue Hospital for examination and later committed to a state hospital for the criminally insane.

The assassination attempt on King won more sympathy in the North than his speeches could have. He was in the hospital for ten days, and all during that time crowds stood vigil outside, singing and praying for his recovery. To many militants who had criticized him, his courage had proved his commitment to the nonviolent principles he had espoused. He was compared to Gandhi. For Martin, his brush with death caused him to think even more about the life and philosophy of the Indian martyr; he wanted to learn more. In February 1959, he and Coretta left for India on a trip sponsored by the American Society of Friends.

The India he found was little different from the country Gandhi had set out to free, except that it was now independent of Britain. It was poor and overpopulated, and in India as anywhere else such conditions lead to social conflict. India was still bitterly divided along caste lines and religious lines, and thousands of people in the lowest castes starved to death every year while those in the highest castes lived in opulence. Gandhi's dream of a truly united India seemed to have died. Further, during his life Gandhi's followers had not always adhered to the non-violent principles he preached. There had been violence. Still, Martin came away with a generally positive view of Gandhi's movement and its effects. He longed to re-create it and improve on it in the United States in a unified movement of committed volunteers who would not succumb to violent urges and who would have total faith in their leader, him.

In the winter of 1959 Martin Luther King, Jr., resigned his pastorship of the Dexter Avenue Baptist Church in Montgomery so he could spend more time working for the SCLC. At long last, he accepted an assistant pastorship in his father's Ebenezer Baptist Church in Atlanta, for he did not want to give up his church work altogether. This would mean moving in on younger brother A. D. King's territory a bit, for his father and A. D. had come to an understanding about their divergent attitudes on life and A.D. now served as assistant pastor. But A.D. was as easy-going as ever; he welcomed Martin's return to Atlanta. By early January, Martin and his family, which now included an infant son, Martin Luther King, III, had settled into a rented house in Atlanta. Relieved of the pressure of a full pastorship, Martin was able to devote more attention to building the SCLC and finding a specific cause behind which the nation's blacks could be united.

Some of the nation's young blacks did not wait for him. Early in 1960, a kind of spontaneous combustion occurred on southern black campuses. The students were tired of segregation and they wanted to do something about it. Two students from Agricultural Technical College of North Carolina decided, single-handedly, to desegregate area lunch counters. They sat at a Woolworth's lunch counter for twelve and a half hours one day, but prompted no reaction; they returned the next day, and the next. News of the action spread by word of mouth, and some students at the white Women's College of the University of North Carolina heard about it. By the fourth day they had joined the black male students sitting in at the Woolworth's lunch counter. The story was picked up by local newspapers and read by students at black North Carolina College and white Duke University in Durham, who started a sit-in at a local restaurant. Within two weeks, college students in four neighboring states had begun their own sit-ins, and a month later ten southern states were involved. The authorities had begun to retaliate, which may partly explain the rapid growth of the college student movement. There was something about mass arrests and rough treatment of fellow students that caused students to unite. And the more arrests and the rougher the treatment, the larger the number of students who joined in.

In Atlanta, Martin Luther King read newspaper reports of the sit-ins and marveled at the students' tenacity. In his experience, college students had been quick to be inspired and just as quick to become bored with a sustained action.

The sit-in movement was different. In his experience, college students had been the most emotionally volatile, the hardest to convince that nonviolence was the best path. But the college students who were sitting in at lunch counters across the South were adhering completely to nonviolent principles. This was the list of rules governing behavior at sit-ins drawn up by Nashville, Tennessee, college students that spring:

> Don't strike back if cursed or abused.
> Don't laugh out.
> Don't hold conversations with your fellow workers.
> Don't leave your seats until your leader has given you instructions to do so.
> Don't block entrances to the stores and the aisles.
> Show yourself courteous and friendly at all times.
> Sit straight and always face the counter.
> Report all serious incidents to your leader.
> Refer all information to your leader in a polite manner.
> Remember love and nonviolence.
> May God bless each of you.

It was strongly reminiscent of the rules King and other leaders of the Montgomery Improvement Association had applied to the Montgomery bus boycott. Clearly, both civil rights activism and nonviolent principles were ideas whose time had come in black southern America. The SCLC sent invitations to sit-in leaders of all ten affected southern states to attend an organizational rally at Shaw University in Raleigh, North Carolina, in April 1960. Out of that rally would emerge the Student Nonviolent Coordinating Committee (SNCC), an organization separate from the SCLC but somewhat dependent on it for guidance. Martin Luther King, Jr., was invited to be SNCC's adviser.

Less than a month later, on May 6, 1960, President Eisenhower signed into law the second civil rights bill since 1875. Once again it had to do with voting rights. Once again it was weak and ineffectual. Unlike the earlier bill, it provided that the Department of Justice could take action on behalf of any person denied the right to register to vote; but the person in question had to prove "a pattern or practice of discrimination," which was frequently difficult, if not impossible. Also, one of its provisions mandated federal prison sentences for persons crossing state lines "to foment violence." Such a vague charge would be as easy for state authorities to prove against civil rights workers as charges of "patterns or practices of discrimination" would be hard to prove against local government in the South. Once again the federal government, deferring to southern legislators, had taken a supposedly strong stand that was actually rooted in quicksand.

Meanwhile, however, small evidences of a chink in the solid armor of the Old South were beginning to appear. Here and there, department store lunch counters were being desegregated without violence and without publicity. Here and there, the "Whites Only" signs were being removed from public drinking fountains. In the same month that the latest civil rights bill was signed into law, Martin Luther King, Jr., personally witnessed another chink in the armor of the South.

A couple of months earlier, King had been indicted for perjury in filing his 1956 and 1958 income tax returns.

(Harassing a black "troublemaker" by questioning his tax returns was a tried and effective method, as black Congressman Adam Clayton Powell, Jr., could already attest.) His trial had been set for May 23, 1960. King entered the court with no hope whatsoever of acquittal. He had not lied on his income tax returns, but in southern courts when the defendant was black and the jury was white, matters of evidence, matters of right and wrong, of true and false testimony, meant little. Thousands of ordinary black men had been found guilty despite a preponderance of facts attesting to their innocence. Martin was no ordinary black man. He heard the star witness testify that the state tax commission had found no evidence of fraud in his tax returns for the years in question, and still he was not optimistic. The trial took six days; the jury was out for four hours. When they came back in, he was resigned, as he had been all the while, to a "Guilty" verdict. When the white foreman said "Not guilty," he went numb. His attorney and his wife burst into tears. He did not. He suddenly felt the overwhelming presence of God in the courtroom. How else could it be explained—the acquittal of a black man by an all-white jury in the South?

Late in the summer of 1960, John F. Kennedy was nominated as the Democratic candidate for President of the United States, and most blacks supported him, for they believed the Democrats were more sympathetic to the common people, including blacks, than the Republicans were. King hoped to gain the ear of the candidate and urge his support of a new and stronger civil rights bill. He had helped stage and had participated in civil rights rallies in Los Angeles, the Democratic convention site, and in other cities during the presidential campaign, hoping to call Kennedy's attention to the civil rights issue. He had,

Martin Luther King, Jr., leads a march through Albany, Georgia, in 1961 on behalf of other jailed blacks. He and 265 others were arrested themselves as a result of the march. (UNITED PRESS INTERNATIONAL.)

in fact, concentrated on the election so much that some of his advisers feared he was moving too far away from the grass roots movement, the sit-ins and boycotts on the local level. In October the Atlanta SNCC group was planning sit-ins at Rich's department store and Walgreen's drugstore. A. D. King was going to participate in the action at Walgreen's. If Martin did not join in the sit-ins, the press would notice it. Anyway, the sit-in movement needed the impetus only King could provide. He agreed to take part in the action at Rich's department store.

The first day of the sit-ins had been labeled "D Day" by the SNCC coordinators. On the morning of D Day, King was driven to Rich's department store. He led the way to

The Early Civil Rights Movement • 71

the store's main dining room, followed by demonstrators who had been picketing outside the store while awaiting his arrival. Within moments after their arrival, store officials called the police and minutes later the squad cars pulled up. King and scores of other sitters-in were dragged out of the store and taken to the police station where they were booked on a charge of violating the city's segregation ordinance.

A few months earlier King had been unjustly arrested on a traffic violation charge. The judge in the case had released him on probation, provided he did not get into any "trouble." His appearance at the sit-in at Rich's department store constituted "trouble," and the Atlanta authorities had a legal basis for throwing the book at King. They intended to sentence him to four months hard labor at Reidsville State Prison. Ordinarily, King's imprisonment would not have been particularly important— after all, he'd been arrested and jailed before. But 1960 was an election year and both John F. Kennedy and his Republican opponent, former Vice President Richard M. Nixon, realized that like it or not, the equal rights struggle was a present force. Nixon issued a statement in support of King. Kennedy went further. Publicly, the only thing he did was to call Coretta King. But he made other private calls to influential people. After one day in jail Martin Luther King, Jr., was free on bond.

Out of jail, King gave credit to Kennedy for his freedom. When Kennedy won the presidential election in November, King and other black leaders claimed that Kennedy had won because of the black vote. But the new President did not thank or acknowledge King. Only his Vice President, Lyndon B. Johnson, wrote a note of thanks.

Chapter 4
The Movement
Matures, and Fades

In April 1961, leaders of the SCLC and another veteran civil rights group, the Congress of Racial Equality (CORE), invited the leaders of SNCC to a meeting to discuss future civil rights actions in the South. The leadership of the two older organizations had been surprised at the tenacity and effectiveness of the student organization, which was financially poor but rich in energy and commitment. SNCC had been highly successful in desegregating lunch counters and other facilities across the South, and SCLC and CORE hoped that a combination of their financial resources and wisdom with SNCC's manpower could be more effective than the work of the three organizations acting independently. At the meeting, it was decided that the next target for desegregation should be interstate buses in the South. Martin Luther King, Jr., was named chairman of the committee to coordinate these actions, which came to be called Freedom Rides.

On May 4 the first two buses, a Trailways and a Greyhound, left Washington, D.C., fifteen minutes apart for a trip through Virginia, North and South Carolina, Georgia, Alabama and Mississippi. All the stops had been planned in advance and federal, state, and local officials notified. At each stop the Freedom Riders, composed of both whites and blacks, planned to debark from the buses and desegregate bus station dining and rest-room facilities. During the first stops, they were comparatively successful. White riders were allowed to use black toilets, black riders white toilets. At some lunch counters they were served, at others they were ignored, but they were not harmed. As they moved farther south, the atmosphere changed.

When the Greyhound bus arrived at Rock Hill, South Carolina, a crowd of whites, behind which stood the police, waited for them to get off. The crowd beat up the first three passengers, one black and two white, before the police stepped in to stop the violence. The buses moved on through South Carolina and Georgia. Outside Anniston, Alabama, the Greyhound bus was attacked by a group of white men wielding two-by-four pine boards. They smashed out the windows and set it afire, and as the passengers emerged coughing and choking from the exits they were beaten. The Trailways bus passed the scene fifteen minutes later, its passengers now aware of what was in store for them and badly frightened.

In the center of Anniston, white men armed with sticks and tire irons boarded the bus and beat the riders, then remained on the bus and ordered the driver to go to Birmingham. At Birmingham, the hoodlums ordered the Freedom Riders to debark. They were savagely beaten by the waiting crowd. The second Freedom Ride bus got no farther than Birmingham. King was ready to give up the Freedom Ride campaign, and so were most of the other leaders. The students felt differently. They prepared to set out in buses from Nashville, Tennessee, for a second Freedom Ride, this time to Montgomery, Alabama. They were far more willing to engage in the politics of confrontation than their elders.

A mob was waiting at the Montgomery bus terminal. They beat the first riders to step off the bus; they beat reporters; they beat an observer sent by the Kennedy Administration. The young militants would not be defeated. They intended to continue on to Jackson, Mississippi. In Washington, the Administration could stand by idly no longer. Federal troops were sent to escort the buses, to protect them from further violence.

SNCC leaders felt triumphant. King despaired. What progress had been made if a handful of Freedom Riders needed 400 soldiers to protect them as they rode through the South? And how could their activities be called a "movement" when the overwhelming majority of American blacks were not personally involved? Despite all the publicity, less than five per cent of the U.S. black population (fewer than one million of the twenty-two million) were actually participating. They were not willing to put their bodies on the line; they had neither the courage nor the recklessness of the young militants, black or white. King understood this, which was why he had hoped to get a massive voter registration drive going. But he just could not seem to arouse the people. SNCC continued its Freedom Rides alone, despite the gradual withdrawal of support from SCLC and CORE. Early in November the Interstate Commerce Commission ruled against segregation on all interstate vehicles and public facilities. In the future, all vehicles and terminals would have posted signs declaring seating "without regard to race, color, creed or national origin." The order was not uniformly obeyed in the South, but gradually the power of law would overcome the power of emotion and tradition.

The tone of the civil rights movement was changing, and Martin Luther King, Jr., had little control over it. He did not support the tactics of confrontation being employed by SNCC and other young militants, and yet those seemed to be the only tactics that worked. They represented a departure from the nonviolent philosophy that King held so dear, but he had to admit they were effective. He and other SCLC leaders hoped to regain control of the movement by adopting the tone of confrontation of the youthful militants publicly, but working to negotiate with the authorities behind the scenes. The city of Birmingham, Alabama, was selected as the site of a massive civil rights crusade in April. The plans were drawn up in secret, but officials of the Kennedy Administration were informed beforehand. King and other leaders of SCLC hoped to win their fight without federal assistance, but if they needed help they wanted to be sure it would be forthcoming.

The Kings' fourth child, Bernice Albertine, was born, but Martin was too busy to be with his wife. He was in Birmingham beginning the crusade that he hoped would bring the civil rights movement back to the nonviolent philosophy. Once again, all demonstrators were urged to refrain from violence "of fist, tongue and heart," and to see the goal of desegregation as a reconciliation with whites rather than a victory over them. Many signed a pledge committing themselves to go to prison. King hoped to pack the Birmingham jails to overflowing.

The crusade began quietly with student sit-ins at a few downtown lunch counters. Over the next few days there were marches and other peaceful demonstrations. There were also many peaceful arrests. As the relatively peaceful atmosphere continued, blacks who had been afraid of possible violence and had refused to become involved joined the original protesters. Seeing the movement grow, the city of Birmingham obtained an injunction against King, the SCLC, and the marchers. Some of King's advisers counseled him to obey the injunction. If their protest was to be peaceful and nonviolent, they should obey the law. King disagreed. If they stopped now, their cause would be lost. On Good Friday, King actually participated in a Birmingham demonstration for the first time, and he was arrested and jailed. He had hoped other clergymen, black and white, would join him, or at least support him. They did not. Most of the city's black ministers remained aloof, and eight leading white ministers and priests issued a public plea to the city's blacks not to support the demonstrations. In jail, King sat down and wrote a letter to his fellow clergymen in which he explained the reasons behind the campaign and defended its tactics, and reminded the ministers of their responsibility to uphold justice and fight injustice. Called "Letter from Birmingham Jail," it became famous, for it identified the basic problem behind all types of social injustice. As he once wrote, "The ultimate tragedy is not the brutality of the bad people but the silence of the good people."

King was in prison for eight days. When he was released, he learned that a new tactic was being planned for the demonstrations. Children would be sent to desegregate public parks and libraries. The authorities could hardly arrest children. A few days later, early one Thursday afternoon, some one thousand children assembled at Birmingham's Sixteenth Street Baptist Church to receive

Martin Luther King, Jr., gazes through the bars of his cell in the Jefferson County Courthouse in Birmingham, Alabama. He understood that he had to make such sacrifices if he was to be a true practitioner and leader of nonviolent protests. While in this jail he wrote his famous "Letter from a Birmingham Jail." (UNITED PRESS INTERNATIONAL)

instructions from King. He asked if they were willing to go to prison. All said "Yes!" Then, in groups of ten to fifty, they dispersed, laughing and dancing off in different directions so as not to arouse police suspicion but planning to assemble for a march through the downtown section. By the time the police realized what was happening, the small groups had met and formed a huge wave that rolled through the streets, blocking traffic at times but otherwise doing nothing to hamper the flow of downtown activity. Once assembled, the children walked solemnly, not laughing or skipping. They understood the seriousness of their mission, and they were suddenly a little bit scared. Television crews and newspaper reporters rushed to the scene. They were there to record police hauling children, some no more than seven or eight years old, into vans and off to jail, police clubbing some of the older boys. It was a major story, this "children's crusade."

The next morning, more than a thousand children assembled in the Sixteenth Street Baptist Church. Learning of the meeting, Sheriff "Bull" Connor sent his men to surround the church and keep the kids from going downtown. This time, the police were accompanied by firemen. As groups of children tried to escape from the exits of the church, the firemen pulled the heavy hoses from their trucks and turned the steam pressure up to full. Blasts of water ripped into the groups of running children, smashing them against fences and down on the sidewalks. Screaming and crying, they tried to escape from the relentless, pounding water. The spectacle was not enough for "Bull" Connor. He ordered his men to release their police dogs. They leaped into the fray, snarling and snapping at the children. Hundreds more were arrested, their clothing drenched, hair plastered to their faces, eyes wide with fear. Television cameras recorded every detail and that evening millions of Americans watched in horror as children were mowed down by the torrents of water and dragged about by ferocious dogs. Satellites carried the pictures all over the world. Birmingham was an international scandal.

The children did what the older demonstrators had been unable to accomplish: they mobilized Birmingham's black adults. Within days so many marches and demonstrations were taking place that even the SCLC coordinators could not keep track of them. And the police were hopelessly unequal to the situation; they would stop one demonstration only to be called to control another. Soon the jails were full for miles around. Outbreaks of violence suddenly occurred. Bands of white vigilantes cruised through the black neighborhoods, attacking lone blacks, bombing black homes. In response, blacks armed with sticks and knives invaded white sections, beating policemen, setting fire to stores and houses. King, Abernathy and others walked through the black neighborhoods pleading for an end to the violence. Some blacks handed over their weapons. The violence subsided as quickly as it had erupted. King and other SCLC leaders met with a group of Birmingham businessmen and an agreement was negotiated which provided for desegregation of store facilities, more jobs for blacks, and biracial committees to look into grievances and solve problems. When the agreement was announced early in May 1962, it was the major news story in the media. It appeared that the Birmingham campaign had been a huge success. On June 11 President John F. Kennedy spoke to the people on national television, calling for the country to fulfill its promise of freedom and equality, and for Congress to pass an effective civil rights bill. It was the strongest commitment to civil rights ever voiced publicly by an American President.

Civil rights leaders wanted to build on the momentum of the President's speech. If they sat back and waited for Congress to take strong action, it would never be taken, they felt. They had to present a show of unity, of numerical power. A. Philip Randolph, president of the black Brotherhood of Sleeping Car Porters, had long wanted to stage a march on Washington, and he thought now was the time to do it. It would be a peaceful demonstration of peaceful people meeting not to demand immediate equality but to encourage the visible progress toward it, to direct national attention to the issue. It was planned for August 28.

More than 200,000 people assembled for the march to the Lincoln Memorial on that day, and a quarter of them were white, a showing that surprised Randolph and the other leaders. They realized the Birmingham "children's crusade," covered so extensively by the media, had caused many white liberals to take a stand on civil rights. They realized, too, that John Kennedy's support of civil rights legislation had helped make it more acceptable to whites. But they still had not expected such support, and they were delighted.

The March on Washington was one of the happiest demonstrations the capital has ever seen. Considerable planning had gone into crowd control and dealing with violence and disorder. None of the plans was necessary. The crowd was friendly, hopeful, enjoying themselves in the bright midday sun. Their spirit was infectious. The speakers caught the sense of hopefulness and expressed it in their words. Martin Luther King, Jr., had written a rather solemn speech, dwelling on the injustices suffered by blacks for three hundred years. But up on the steps of the Lincoln Memorial, looking out over the sea of expectant white and black faces, he changed his mind, and spoke from his heart the words for which he is best remembered:

"I say to you today, my friends, that in spite of the difficulties and frustrations of the moment I still have a dream. It is a dream deeply rooted in the American dream. I have a dream that one day this nation will rise up and live out the true meaning of its creed: 'We hold these truths to be self-evident; that *all* men are created equal.' I have a dream . . ."

The crowd was electrified. As King's voice thundered across the mall, it was answered by cheers and amens, and with each "I have a dream—" 200,000 hearts were lifted higher.

"I have a dream that one day even the state of Mississippi, a desert state sweltering with the heat of injustice and oppression, will be transformed into an oasis of freedom and justice.

"I have a dream that my four little children will one day live in a nation where they will not be judged by the color of their skin but by the content of their character.

"I have a dream . . . I have a dream . . . I have a dream . . ." He had the crowd mesmerized. Their souls lifted and soared with the cadence of his voice, with the repetition, over and over, of that phrase. And then he introduced a new phrase: "Let freedom ring," he shouted, his voice reverberating like the Liberty Bell itself.

"When we let freedom ring, when we let it ring from every village and every hamlet, from every state and every city, we will be able to speed up that day when *all* of God's children, black men and white men, Jews and Gen-

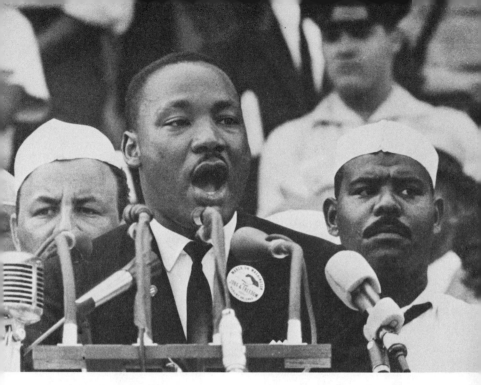

Martin Luther King, Jr., delivers his famous "I Have a Dream" speech at the Lincoln Memorial in Washington, D.C., on August 28, 1963. It is among the most widely quoted speeches in modern times. (UNITED PRESS INTERNATIONAL)

tiles, Protestants and Catholics, will be able to join hands and sing in the words of the old Negro spiritual, 'Free at last! free at last! thank God Almighty, we are free at last!' "

It took the crowd a full minute to react. They were literally speechless. When they found their voices, they went wild, yelling and stomping for joy. Many wept openly. At that moment they felt a collective soul force so strong that they could not imagine America's failing them. How could Congress not respond to those words and pass a strong civil rights law? How could the most racist white not be

The Movement Matures, and Fades · 83

uplifted by that God-like voice? But the euphoria did not last long. Freedom would not ring throughout the land. A mourning bell would toll across a nation mired in violence and hatred.

On Sunday September 15, 1963, the Sixteenth Street Baptist Church in Birmingham was bombed, killing four little girls who were attending Sunday school. Hopes for an end to white racist violence were crushed—tragically. The veritable murder of black children in a house of worship showed just how far the South had yet to travel on the path toward peaceful coexistence between the races. Black Americans had just begun to recover from the shock of this senseless killing when another and more far-reaching tragedy occurred. On November 22, John F. Kennedy, who had inspired the admiration and loyalty of black America more than any other President since Abraham Lincoln, was assassinated in Dallas, Texas. While in police custody, his assassin, Lee Harvey Oswald, was himself murdered by a Dallas restaurant owner named Jack Ruby. Martin Luther King, Jr., sat in front of the television set in his home in Atlanta, watching the replay of these events and the coverage of the slain President's funeral, and despaired that the rage and hostility that seemed to grip the country would ever end.

Several hundred miles to the north, in Jefferson City, Missouri, inmates of the Missouri State Penitentiary also watched the television coverage and discussed the Kennedy assassination. Several prisoners stated their certainty that Lee Harvey Oswald had been paid to do the killing. "The man who murders King will make another million," someone said. "That's the million I want to collect," said James Earl Ray.

His fellow inmates must have looked at Ray with some

incredulity and chuckled under their breath. There he was, talking big again. He could not even pull a simple robbery without being caught. In the Missouri criminal world, he was known as "the commuter" because he had been in and out of prison so frequently. And yet, he never seemed to accept his ineptness at crime. He was always talking about some grandiose scheme or other, schemes that either never materialized or were hopelessly botched. James Earl Ray seemed a natural-born loser.

In many ways, he was just that. Born on March 10, 1928, to an ex-convict father and an alcoholic mother, James had grown up on a farm in Ewing, Missouri, in grinding poverty. He had dropped out of high school in the tenth grade, had been court-martialed and imprisoned for being drunk and disorderly while in the army, and had been discharged before his period of service was completed. A problem drinker, he was unable to hold a steady job after his discharge and soon turned to crime, robbing supermarkets and all-night cafeterias. He was invariably caught: he dropped pieces of identification at the scene of a crime, he got drunk and returned to places he had robbed, he forgot to use different handwriting on the front and back of stolen money orders.

He spent a lot of time in prison, but he developed no real friendships with his fellow inmates, who were contemptuous of him because of his farm origins and his ineptness at crime. They did not take seriously his constant talk of escaping or his plans for big robberies. He did do business with his fellow prisoners, though. Ray was a clever prison entrepreneur, and every time he was in prison for a sufficient period he established an underground commerce in food, cigarettes and, some say, even drugs, managing to make a substantial profit for himself.

Coretta and the Kings' four children, (left to right) Yolanda
Denise, Bernice Albertine, Dexter Scott, and Martin Luther III,
in 1964. Because of his busy schedule, Dr. King had little time
to spend with his family. (UNITED PRESS INTERNATIONAL)

86 · The Life and Death of Martin Luther King, Jr.

In fact, he was far more successful inside than outside, where his cleverness seemed to desert him. By November 1963 he had been in Jefferson City prison for some three and a half years of a twenty-year sentence for armed robbery. He had made two attempts to escape and had failed miserably both times. He was doing a highly successful black-market business, however, facilitated by his having secured a work assignment in the prison bakery, where he could obtain food items to sell to his fellow inmates. Meanwhile he dreamed of escaping and, once on the outside, of committing a successful major crime that would net him a lot of money.

On the outside, the civil rights movement continued. The Student Nonviolent Coordinating Committee decided to conduct a massive voter registration drive in Mississippi and Alabama in the summer of 1964. In June hundreds of students, black and white, converged on the states, fanning out into the small towns and hamlets where blacks were most timid and whites seemed to be most fearlessly cruel. Hundreds of the workers were arrested and jailed; scores were beaten senseless by angry whites in and out of uniform. But the only way the workers could show the poor black farmers how important the vote was to them was to put their lives on the line, and they did so, time and again.

CORE also planned an action in Mississippi that summer, a People-to-People March to dramatize the voter registration drive. In June two young white CORE workers, Andrew Goodman and Michael Schwerner, traveled to Mississippi to look over the area and were shown around by a black Mississippi civil rights worker named James Chaney. In the small town of Philadelphia, Mississippi, their car was pulled over by local deputies and the three were arrested for speeding. They were never heard from again. For weeks a 200-man search party combed the area, and FBI agents sought clues to the whereabouts of the three young men. In August their bodies were found in the mud of a dam built across the Tallahala River near Philadelphia. Twenty-one men, one of whom confessed that they were a Ku Klux Klan lynching party, were indicted, but the state of Mississippi would not try them for the murder and the federal government could not (murder is not a federal crime). Charges against the men were dismissed.

In September 1964, Martin Luther King, Jr., was awarded the Nobel Prize for Peace, to become only the second black American so honored. Eight members of the Norwegian Parliament had decided that as the foremost leader of the nonviolent movement for black equality in the United States during 1964, he deserved the prize more than any other world leader, and in awarding him the prize they raised him to the level of a world, rather than a national, leader. Yet, two months later the Director of the FBI, J. Edgar Hoover, called him "the most notorious liar in the country," and the statement made headlines. Hoover would never go into detail about what he meant, but subsequent remarks about civil rights leaders as "communists" and "moral degenerates" were clearly aimed at King. Without specific allegations to bolster it, however, the furor died down. Besides, King was due to go to Norway to accept the Nobel prize, and it was not in the best interests of America to keep the story alive.

By the beginning of the new year, SNCC had made considerable progress in registering black voters in Alabama and otherwise increasing their militancy against segregation. It was decided to stage another campaign of

Martin hugs Coretta after learning that he has been awarded the 1964 Nobel Prize for Peace. (UNITED PRESS INTERNATIONAL)

demonstrations in Selma, Alabama, and insiders were predicting another Birmingham. King and other SCLC leaders went to Selma hoping to prevent that, to keep the lines of communication to the white authorities open, to keep the demonstrations and marches nonviolent. Once again King decided to stuff the jails. On Monday, February 1, he and Abernathy led some 750–800 people, most of whom were schoolchildren, in a march on the Selma courthouse to dramatize the voter registration drive. All were arrested and jailed. Within days, the jails were indeed packed to bursting. The police were getting short-tempered. On

The Movement Matures, and Fades · 89

February 10, cars and trucks carrying Sheriff Jim Clark and his deputies surrounded a group of about 150 children demonstrating in the downtown area of Selma and drove them like cattle out of town, forcing them to trot along the country roads and laughing and prodding them when they could not keep up the pace. Just as in Birmingham, angry black parents became militant civil rights activists overnight, and press and television coverage caused Selma, Alabama, to be equated with horror and white brutality in the eyes of the world.

Hundreds of civil rights activists, black and white, converged on Selma, and suddenly the police had to deal with, of all things, rioting nuns from Chicago! Taking advantage of the influx of supporters, King announced a march from Selma to Montgomery on March 7. In response, Alabama Governor George Wallace sent state police against the marchers, and once again television watchers saw scenes of incredible white police brutality against unarmed citizens. Two days later, President Lyndon Johnson sent federal troops to Alabama.

Vice President Lyndon Baines Johnson had assumed the presidency two hours after the death of President Kennedy. The big, strapping Texan had been in an awkward position, for he was assuming the office under a cloud, and taking over from such a sophisticated and popular man with an attractive young family would have been difficult under any circumstances. He had hastened to assure the nation that he would continue Kennedy's programs and policies, and in the area of civil rights he would prove to be far more committed than even Kennedy had been.

A week after he took office, he summoned civil rights leaders to the White House for discussions on a Kennedy bill that was stalled in the House of Representatives. Soon,

Standing before a map of the United States on which the target cities of the SCLC's drive against segregation are charted, Martin Luther King, Jr., points to Selma, Alabama, where a three-pronged attack against racial barriers is planned. (UNITED PRESS INTERNATIONAL)

he had begun to exercise his personal influence to push the bill through, and in 1964 he had signed it into law. But this bill, like others before it, had not provided sufficient funds or clout for its enforcement, and it had been too general to open the way for any significant rights gains for blacks. After Selma, Lyndon Johnson realized that more specific legislation was needed, especially specific voting rights legislation. He ordered the Justice Department to draft a strong Voting Rights Act, and when it was ready he personally presented the bill to a joint session of Congress, in a speech that was televised over the major networks.

"I speak tonight," he began, "for the dignity of man and the destiny of democracy. . . . There is no constitutional issue here. The command of the Constitution is plain. There is no moral issue. It is wrong . . . to deny any of your fellow Americans the right to vote. . . . What happened in Selma is part of a far larger movement which reaches into every section and every state of America. It is the effort of American Negroes to secure for themselves the full blessings of American life. Their cause must be our cause, too. Because it is not just Negroes, but really it is all of us who must overcome the crippling legacy of bigotry and injustice. And . . . we . . . shall . . . overcome!" Martin Luther King, Jr., heard and saw the speech on television and was moved. He told reporters that it "revealed great and amazing understanding of the depth of the problem of racial injustice." On August 6, 1965, President Johnson signed into law the Voting Rights Act of 1965, a law which, with the courageous efforts of thousands of civil rights workers, provided the basis for the current political potency of blacks in the South.

On August 11, 1965, in Watts, a suburb of Los Angeles, a black man named Marquette Frye was pulled over for speeding. Not normally a drinker (because he couldn't hold his liquor very well) Frye had been drinking that day. Still, he was not particularly belligerent, and the officer, Lee Minekus, was not overreacting when he switched on his two-way radio and called for a motorcycle officer and a sheriff's car; it was normal procedure to call for such assistance in transporting an "intoxicated driver" to the county station and taking charge of the area where the arrest occurred. Unfortunately, August 11, 1965, was a slow day for the police; too many responded. Unfortunately, August 11, 1965, was a slow day in Watts; too many passers-by stopped to watch, and as more police cars arrived more people came to watch. Perhaps nothing would have happened if the principals in the arrest had not suddenly found themselves faced with such a large audience; perhaps the spectators would not have acted if their numbers had not been so great. No one is sure how it started or who started it, but suddenly suspect and police were fighting, the crowd had turned into a mob, and the Watts riot had begun—days of looting and burning as some of the residents took out years of pent-up frustration on the nearest target available, their own neighborhood. It shocked the country, and it shocked the major civil rights leaders, among them Martin Luther King, Jr.

King realized that while he and other leaders had been concentrating on the South, they had neglected the blacks of the North, who suffered under another kind of discrimination and segregation, a more insidious kind. While they might be able to eat in some public restaurants and use public facilities, they were effectively excluded from many others because they could not afford them. They might not live under actual segregated housing laws, but they were nevertheless confined to ghettos far less benign than the scattered black sections of southern towns. Theoretically, their children might not go to segregated schools, but somehow they went to all-black schools just the same. In the South, for all its faults, there was a certain "live and let live," courteous attitude that was not present in the North. Martin Luther King, Jr., decided that the civil rights movement was needed by northern blacks nearly as much as by their southern brethren, and early in 1966 he decided to take his nonviolent crusade to Chicago.

Dr. King was a forceful speaker, and at no time was he more forceful than when he spoke of the need for black civil rights. (UNITED PRESS INTERNATIONAL)

The purpose of the campaign was to call attention to and bring improvements in the substandard ghetto housing in which most Chicago blacks lived, to obtain a higher minimum wage (for most of the city's blacks worked at minimum wage jobs), and to bring about public school desegregation. King moved into a slum apartment on Chicago's west side and began taking long walks through the neighborhood, accompanied by the press, during which he pointed out housing code violations and talked about the despair that drove poor people doomed to low-paying jobs to go on welfare, the high unemployment rate among blacks, and the lack of adequate nutrition.

These walks did cause the city's building code inspectors to visit the area and to charge some slum landlords with violations. Unwilling to face bad publicity, other slum landlords made repairs, did repainting and in other ways tried to make their buildings more livable. But this minor progress could hardly be called a successful movement, and when in the middle of February the west side ghetto erupted with rioting and looting, King's SCLC staff was accused of purposely bringing disorder to the city. King was able to persuade Chicago's Mayor Daley to have sprinklers installed on fire hydrants, to request federal funds for more swimming pools, and to appoint a committee to counsel the police department on how to improve its community relations, but these could hardly be called major victories. Certainly King had failed to convince the majority of Chicagoans that they could significantly improve their lives through nonviolent demonstrations.

In March 1966 James Earl Ray tried for the third time to escape from Jefferson City Prison. First he shaped his blankets to resemble his sleeping form, then climbed a metal pole to a high window in his cell. Using a pair of stolen wire cutters, he cut a hole in the wire mesh covering the window and crawled through it to the top of an interior wall. A few feet away was a fan ventilator. He climbed inside it and waited for an opportune moment to make his way to an outer wall from which he could drop down to the street. His absence was discovered within thirty minutes, and for nearly thirty hours the guards searched for him. With the prison swarming with guards and the sentries alerted, Ray had little chance to make his move. Late the following night he crawled out of the ventilator and gave himself up.

In June 1966, James Meredith, the first black student

ever to enroll in the University of Mississippi, decided to test the theory that the South was now a free and safe place for the black man. With three friends, he set out from the Tennessee border along Highway 51 to walk the 210 miles to Jackson, Mississippi. It would be a long trek along many isolated stretches of road, but Meredith felt he had to find out one way or the other if freedom had come to Mississippi. On the first day, a shotgun blast came from a group of shrubs next to the road, and felled James Meredith. Although Meredith was not seriously injured, civil rights leaders and workers across the country were enraged. They converged on Memphis, Tennessee, where Meredith had been taken to the hospital, and announced that they would continue the young man's march.

The march marked the public shift in the philosophy of the civil rights movement, and the public split among its various leaders. SNCC led the way. They were tired of nonviolence. It had not shamed many whites into treating blacks humanely, and it had made it easier for some to be even more violent. After the Mississippi summer of 1964, after Birmingham and Selma, after years of being beaten and arrested and jailed, they were no longer in a loving, forgiving mood. They were not sure they wanted integration anymore. All they wanted were equal rights, and they were convinced they had to seize those rights. SNCC President Stokely Carmichael insisted that the march make a stop at Greenwood, Mississippi, where he had once been arrested. There, he stood before the six hundred marchers and issued his now famous call for "Black Power!" Within a few days CORE had accepted the slogan and the militant posture it implied. The SCLC and the NAACP were no longer in charge of the civil rights movement. The young militants were willing to give them credit for many past civil rights gains, but the general attitude was that their time had passed and they must make way for new blood and new ideas. The old leaders had started the movement and seen it through its first stages; with maturity the movement needed new direction.

Martin Luther King, Jr., was not ready to be a has-been. He was still the most well-known and respected black leader in the country and he intended to maintain that position, despite the fact that he was losing control of the civil rights movement. Just as he had chosen the voting rights issue as his cause some years before, he would choose a new cause now. For many years he had been thinking about enlarging the scope of his nonviolent philosophy, applying it not just to the human rights struggle of blacks in the United States but to the cause of world peace. After he had been awarded the Nobel Peace Prize, he had begun to feel that he was in a position to be listened to. In the spring of 1965 he had spoken out publicly against the escalating war in Vietnam and prompted considerable adverse reaction. Realizing he could hurt the cause of the civil rights movement, particularly the chances of a strong voting rights act, he had not pressed the issue. Now, however, he was in many ways a leader without a movement. He was deeply disturbed by increased American involvement in Vietnam and by U. S. support of a puppet government in South Vietnam not representative of the mass of its people. He believed he could combine the fight for civil rights with the struggle for world peace. This would be his cause. Unfortunately, in pursuing his anti-war stand he would have to criticize the very President who had done the most to advance the civil rights of black people.

Lyndon B. Johnson was as determined to help South

Vietnam win its war against North Vietnam as he had been committed to getting strong federal civil rights laws on the books. He believed South Vietnam represented an oasis of democracy in an area of the world that was steadily being taken over by Communism, and he felt it was the duty of the United States to preserve that oasis. Under the Kennedy Administration, military advisers and equipment had been supplied to South Vietnam, but over the years North Vietnam, aided by weapons and advisers from the Soviet Union and Communist China, had made territorial gains and in response American fighting men had also been committed to the war. The majority of these soldiers were draftees, and the majority of those were black. College students could get student deferments, but most blacks did not go to college and could not escape the draft. King began to criticize publicly the fact that while blacks constituted only ten percent of the population, they made up forty percent of the American fighting force in Vietnam, and to ask why they should fight for a country in which they were unable to attend school with whites. He spoke at anti-war rallies in various parts of the country warning that a confrontation between the United States and China in Vietnam could lead to World War III and urging a negotiated settlement. He also questioned the moral right of the United States to intervene in what was essentially another country's civil war.

He was roundly criticized for his statements. Older black leaders felt he was wrong to try to involve the civil rights movement with the anti-war movement. Southern and conservative whites called him a communist, and plenty of other whites resented his public criticism of the United States government. One day in Atlanta he found

Dr. King speaks at an anti-war demonstration outside the United Nations in April 1967. He was criticized for his anti-war crusade by both whites and blacks who felt he was weakening the civil rights crusade. (UNITED PRESS INTERNATIONAL)

an envelope on his desk containing photographs of himself and tape recordings of his conversations in situations which, if made public, would seriously damage his reputation. There was no note with the material, but the message was clear. If he did not stop his campaign against U. S. involvement in the war, the material would be made public. In the past, his advisers had warned King that his telephones and motel rooms might be bugged, but he had not heeded the warnings. Now he realized he'd been spied on for years, probably by the FBI, for what other organi-

The Movement Matures, and Fades · 99

zation had the resources to do it? Still, he refused to be frightened away from a stand which, as a winner of the Nobel Prize for Peace and as a minister, he felt was the only morally correct one to take. In August 1967 he would announce a nationwide campaign to get voters to sign petitions calling for a referendum on the question of American involvement in the war.

James Earl Ray was successful in his fourth attempt to escape from Jefferson City Prison. On April 23, 1967, with the help of some fellow prisoners, he hid in a storage box for bread to be taken to the inmates at a nearby prison farm. Soon after the truck had left the prison grounds, he pried off the lid and, after seven years in prison, was free. When the Missouri prison authorities discovered his escape, they announced a fifty-dollar reward for information leading to his whereabouts or capture. It seems a very small amount for a convicted burglar serving a twenty-year sentence in the state penitentiary, and a minuscule amount for a man who, just over a year later, would be the subject of the largest manhunt in history.

Northern cities erupted in mass race riots in the summer of 1967. Detroit, Michigan, Newark, New Jersey, Harlem in New York were the scenes of looting, burning, and black violence. The civil rights movement had done nothing to better their lives and civil rights leaders had no influence over them. In fact, there were no leaders with influence over them, and the riots were not a movement but a destructive expression of frustration and anger with no other goal but expression. King stayed away from the riot-torn cities, for he knew there was nothing he could do. He was afraid that the civil rights movement had ended. Within a few months, however, he was certain that it

This is the photograph James Earl Ray had taken for his Canadian passport, issued under the name Ramon George Sneyd. (UNITED PRESS INTERNATIONAL TELEPHOTO)

could be resurrected, as part of a new and larger movement of poor people of all races.

Black people's basic, legal rights had been or were being taken care of by law. But they were still prevented from equally enjoying the unalienable right to "the pursuit of happiness" because they were poor and thus ill-educated, neglected medically, undernourished. King realized that they were no different from other poor people in that respect. The time was ripe, he felt, for a national poor people's movement to alert the government and the rest of the country to their plight. Excitedly, he proposed to the other members of SCLC a Poor People's March on Washington the following spring, and on December 4 he made the announcement to the world. The people would march for jobs, for a guaranteed income for everyone not able to work, for a sort of economic Bill of Rights. He would hope to mobilize some three thousand marchers from across the country, he told reporters.

In the next few months he crisscrossed the country urging poor people to join the march. Inspired by him, so many agreed to go to Washington that he realized three thousand people would be needed as marshals alone. Meanwhile, he had taken to preaching every Sunday at Ebenezer Baptist Church. For some years, actually ever since he had given up the pastorship of the Dexter Avenue Baptist Church in Montgomery, he had been far more involved in various movements than in church work. But lately he had shown more interest in his responsibilities to the church; his father was in semiretirement, A. D. had a church of his own, and Martin was aware of the long family tradition of association with Ebenezer Baptist Church. Besides, it represented a solid base where he could turn when his support in other areas waned. One Sunday in February, 1968, he chose as the subject of his sermon his own death, and how he would like to be remembered: "I'd like somebody to mention that day that Martin Luther King, Jr., tried to give his life serving others," he said. "I'd like somebody to say that day that Martin Luther King, Jr., tried to love somebody."

Part 2
The Death of
Martin Luther King, Jr.

Chapter 5
The Assassination

As April 1968, the month of the Poor People's March, approached, King's usually busy schedule became hectic. He seemed to live on airplanes and to spend all his time working out details for the march, details that had grown into major logistical problems. He really did not have time to visit Memphis, Tennessee, to attend a protest march by striking sanitation workers, but he said he would do it anyway. He found it hard to turn down such invitations, especially when they came from friends like the Reverend Billy Kyles. The march was scheduled for March 28, and before he left for Memphis, King knew quite a bit about the background of the protest. Back at the end of January it had rained hard in Memphis one Wednesday morning, so hard that sanitation department officials decided to call in the garbage trucks, manned mostly by blacks, after only two hours. That Friday was a pay day. The black sanitationmen were paid for only two hours' work the previous Wednesday; the white sanitationmen were paid for a full day's work. The black sanitation workers went on strike, demanding not only full pay for the rainy day but eight other considerations: recognition of their union, establishment of a biracial grievance committee, a fair system of promotion without regard to race, insurance benefits for workers, a pension system, sick pay and vacation pay, and a wage increase. Several days later the sanitation workers staged a peaceful march along Main Street. Memphis police overreacted, beating marchers, spraying Mace, a chemical irritant, in their faces. The police actions united the Memphis black community behind the strike and turned it into a protest against the larger racial situation in the city. But within their unity there was much disunity. Many young blacks favored violent confrontation; most older blacks did not. By the time Martin Luther King, Jr., arrived for the March 28th march, Memphis was a racial powder keg, waiting for one spark to set it off.

Martin walked at the front of the long line of black marchers, a big grin on his face. Suddenly he was pushed forward. He turned to see a grim-faced black teen-ager. Along the curbs other young blacks, many armed with sticks and carrying "Black Power!" signs, were moving in on the marchers, trying to break up the demonstration. The police started to move in on them. Soon the streets were filled with fighting blacks and whites; store windows were shattered and their contents looted. A planned non-violent march had dissolved into violence. Martin's friend and bodyguard Bernard Lee decided the situation was too dangerous and hustled him away. Safe in a motel room, King watched television film clips of the march. They clearly showed that black teen-agers were the instigators of the violence. A tremendous setback would be suffered for the nonviolent civil rights movement unless that image could be erased from the public mind. He asked the leaders of the Memphis march to announce that he would lead a peaceful protest march through Memphis within a week. His advisers didn't like the idea. They did not have a solid organization in Memphis and could not take their usual security precautions. Besides, the young militants just could not be counted on. But King was adamant. He felt his own reputation as a civil rights leader was at stake, as was the entire nonviolent philosophy of the civil rights movement.

On March 29, 1968, James Earl Ray walked into the Aeromarine Supply Company in Birmingham, Alabama. He wanted to purchase a high-powered rifle with a scope, he told the clerk, for he thought he might go hunting with his brother. He paid cash for the rifle and scope and signed his name Harvey Lowmyer. The following day he returned. His brother had told him he had bought the wrong gun, he said. He exchanged the rifle for another. A day or two later he set out for Memphis, Tennessee, in the white Mustang he had also purchased in Birmingham. Arriving in Memphis on April 3, he registered as John L. Willard at the New Rebel Motel and paid in advance to stay there from April 3 to April 7.

On April 3, King and Abernathy caught an early morning plane to Memphis. Aboard the plane, they were told by a crew member that there had been a bomb threat and the craft had been under guard all day. Some of King's staff wished he had accepted the offer of protection extended by the Memphis police. But King, as was his custom, had refused, believing that a preacher of nonviolence should not be guarded by police. Neither he nor his staff realized that plainclothes officers had been detailed to watch him closely during his stay in Memphis.

At Memphis airport a car was waiting to drive them

through the cold morning drizzle to the Lorraine Motel on Mulberry Street. King would occupy Room 306, a second-floor room that, like all the other rooms, faced the parking lot and the swimming pool. He could step out on the balcony, which ran the length of the floor, and call to his staff, who had the rooms next door and directly above and below him. They went immediately to work planning for the march, which King had decided to hold on the following Monday, April 8. King went to a meeting of all the black ministers in the area, then returned to the motel where he ordered fish for lunch. Late in the afternoon, leaders of the Invaders, a militant black gang suspected of having caused the earlier march to become violent, arrived for a meeting. King wanted their assurance that they would not disrupt the coming march; he wanted their help in ensuring that nothing would go wrong.

That evening Abernathy and another SCLC member, the Reverend Jesse Jackson, drove through the rain to attend the first meeting designed to gather support for the march, at the Mason Street Temple. King had elected to remain at the motel. He had some calls to make. One was to Marion Logan, a top SCLC fund-raiser and wife of Dr. Arthur Logan, his physician whenever he was in New York. Neither she nor her husband supported the Memphis march, and King was trying to persuade them to do so. He was unsuccessful. The Logans felt that he should not get involved with a labor strike. Besides, they were worried about him. For too many months he had been working obsessively, unable to sleep. They had watched the earlier Memphis march, had seen him at the head of the line while glass shattered behind him, bewildered, not knowing what to do. He couldn't hope to control the situation. "If you don't get out of there, you're going to get yourself killed, Martin," Marion Logan said. Sadly he replied, "Marion, I've been trying to tell you darling, I'm ready to die." She did not take him seriously, and she had not meant, literally, that he would get himself killed. Soon after, King answered a call from Abernathy. Some two thousand people had braved the driving rain to be at the temple, expecting King to be the one who spoke. It wasn't fair to disappoint them. King agreed to go to the temple.

Not expecting to speak, he had not prepared written remarks. Taking the podium at the Mason Street Temple, he looked out over the expectant faces of his audience. He began talking about the impending march, and after a while he remarked that he thanked God that he was there to lead the march. He was speaking extemporaneously, and the remark about his own presence seemed to spark a verbal rumination about the precariousness of his life. Lately, his friends and advisers had noticed, he had been particularly restless and jumpy, starting at sudden noises and movements, looking behind him as if he thought he was being watched or followed. He told of his near assassination in New York and of the threats on his life he had received during the crusades in Birmingham and Selma, of the bomb threat on his plane to Memphis. "And then I got to Memphis," he said, and the crowd laughed, because his tone suggested that despite all the threats he was a man who "kept on keeping on." But the crowd did not laugh as he continued:

"And *some* began to talk about the threats that were out, of what would happen to me from some of our sick white brothers . . ." He paused. "Well, I don't know what *will* happen now. We've got some difficult days ahead. But it really doesn't matter to me now." He paused again. "Because I've been to the *mountaintop!*" he cried.

His voice dropped. "Like anybody I would like to live . . . a long life. Longevity has its place. But I'm not *concerned* about that now. . . ." His voice rose again. "I just want to do *God's* will! And *He's* allowed me to go up to the mountain, and I've *seen* the *Promised Land.*" His voice lowered once more. "I may not get there with you, but I want you to know, tonight," he cried, "that we as a people will get to the Promised Land! So I'm happy tonight, I'm not worried about *anything!* I'm not fearing *any* man! Mine eyes have *seen the glory* of the *coming* of the *Lord!*"

The audience leaped to its feet, stomping, cheering under the electric spell at which King was a twentieth-century master, but those who knew him best realized that this was a highly unusual speech, and that he had never before spoken with such deep feeling about himself. King had exhausted himself giving the speech. All he wanted to do was return to the Lorraine Motel and go to bed.

At noon on April 4, John L. Willard, alias James Earl Ray, checked out of the New Rebel Motel. That morning he had asked a motel employee to bring him a copy of a Memphis newspaper; its front-page story was King's arrival in the city and it carried a photograph of King outside his room at the Lorraine Motel. In the late afternoon Ray, still using the name John L. Willard, registered at Mrs. Brewer's rooming house at 422½ South Main Street. He requested a room at the back. The back of the house faced the courtyard of the Lorraine Motel, about two hundred yards away. Later that afternoon he left the rooming house and went to the nearby York Arms Company, purchased a pair of binoculars, and returned to his room.

For King, Thursday April 4 was filled with meetings and strategy sessions for the upcoming march. King and Abernathy ate lunch at the motel; in the afternoon Abernathy took a nap. They had a long evening ahead of them. First they would go to a soul food dinner at the home of the Reverend Billy Kyles, the organizer of the first march. After that, there was another mass meeting scheduled at the Mason Street Temple.

King was notorious for his habitual lateness, and Kyles had told him that supper would be at five o'clock knowing that King would not manage to get there until six o'clock. At six o'clock King had just finished dressing. The Reverends Jesse Jackson and Andrew Young were in the parking lot, standing beside the waiting limousine. Kyles was standing partway down the stairway. King went out onto the balcony to give some last-minute instructions about the night's meeting. Abernathy stood in the doorway behind him. Then King made a move to return to Room 306. "Oh, Doc—" said Jackson. King bent forward to look down over the balcony railing. A crack split the air and Abernathy fell to the floor. For a moment he thought King, too, had dived for cover. Then he saw the position of his friend's body. The bullet had hit him with such force that it had knocked him flat on his back. Men rushed to him, hoping he was still alive, but he had been dead by the time he hit the balcony floor. All around the courtyard people stood screaming or moaning. Someone called for an ambulance. Police and firemen arrived. All was horror and confusion. A radio station carried a special bulletin: Dr. Martin Luther King, Jr., had been shot at the Lorraine Motel.

Across the motel parking lot, two hundred yards from

The courtyard of the Lorraine Motel in Memphis, where Martin Luther King, Jr., was shot as he stood on the second-floor balcony on the evening of April 4, 1968. (UNITED PRESS INTERNATIONAL)

the balcony, Charles Stephens, a roomer on the second floor of Mrs. Brewer's rooming house, was on his way to the bathroom when a man emerged from a room down the hall. He was carrying a long, bulky bundle. When he saw Stephens, he put his hand up to shield his face. "That sounded like a shot," said Stephens. "Yes," said the man, "it was," as he disappeared down the back staircase.

A few doors down Main Street, a store owner and two customers watched a slim, dark-haired white man drop two bundles in front of the store's recessed window. He then got into a white Mustang and drove north on Main Street. Minutes later a policeman came running up the street. The store owner pointed to the bundles. Minutes after that the rooming house was aswarm with police, for witnesses to the shooting had all pointed to that direction as the origin of the shot. Charles Stephens excitedly reported his encounter in the second-floor hallway with a man carrying a long bundle. One of the bundles dropped in front of the store proved to be a high-powered rifle wrapped in an old green bedspread. The store owner reported that the man he saw had driven off in a white Mustang. Soon Memphis police radios were buzzing with the report: a white man in a white Mustang was being sought in connection with the King shooting.

At St. Joseph's hospital, doctors worked feverishly over King. They performed a tracheotomy. They probed for the bullet. For a while the heart monitor registered some weak impulses, but everyone knew it was useless to go on. The bullet had severed King's spinal cord. He was officially pronounced dead at 7:05 P.M. He had sometimes told his advisers, "I'll never live to be forty. I'll never make it." He had not made it; he was thirty-nine years old.

By 7:05 p.m. Memphis police had a name and a general description of their suspect. He had registered at Mrs. Brewer's earlier that afternoon, signing the register as John L. Willard, insisting on a back room, and paying for a week in advance. Quiet and unassuming, he was tall, slim, dark-haired, with a long thin nose. No one remembered much else about him. The police paid close attention to the description, less to the name. It was most likely an alias. It would be nearly a month before they would know his real name, but by that time they and the FBI would know much more than just his name. They would know a great deal about James Earl Ray.

Chapter 6
The Aftermath

Like tragically too many other dates in our recent history, April 4, 1968, became a day of infamy: a day on which an American in public life was killed by another American. For the majority of the population, reaction to the news was one of shock and disbelief. They switched on their television sets and stared at the images on the screen and listened to the solemn voices of the reporters, trying to comprehend what had happened, wondering what kind of country could kill its best and brightest leaders. For other Americans, the news had little impact. They shrugged their shoulders and muttered, "Well, he had it coming to him. Serves him right for trying to start trouble." Still others rejoiced. White racists hoped the end of King would also mean the end of the civil rights movement. Some black militants hoped fervently that King's death would cause massive retaliation in the cities and that the open guerrilla warfare they encouraged would indeed occur. Authorities in cities across the country feared it would. Curfews were ordered in many areas.

In Memphis, a 7:30 p.m. curfew was declared city-wide, but that did not forestall a wild night of looting and burning. By midnight eighty persons had been arrested and National Guard troops ringed the city. Similar disturbances broke out in some one hundred thirty other cities. Within the space of a single day millions of dollars' worth of property damage occurred and over thirty people (mostly blacks) lost their lives. But the flare-up of violence was comparatively brief. Once their rage had been expressed, blacks settled down to mourn King quietly, to wait and see what the authorities would do to find the killer.

Coretta King and her four children arrived in Memphis the next day, having been flown from Atlanta by an Electra Jet chartered by Senator Robert Kennedy. The funeral was planned for Tuesday April 9, but before Mrs. King returned to Atlanta with her husband's body there were things to do in Memphis. The nonviolent march King had planned was held that Monday as scheduled and became a memorial march for the slain leader. His widow walked in her husband's place at the head of the marchers. Then she accompanied his body to Atlanta where, on Tuesday, it was carried through the streets of the city on a mule-drawn farm wagon, followed by hundreds of thousands of mourners. Mrs. King had chosen a very fitting way to honor her husband, who had tried to represent the simple, common people and whose largest base of support had come from among them.

Meanwhile, all America waited for news of developments in the search for King's killer or killers, and there was wide and varied speculation about whether the crime had been committed by one man acting alone or by a group of conspirators. Majority opinion favored the conspiracy theory, for it was hard to believe that one man could have pulled it off. Within minutes after the shot, the area had been swarming with police and firemen. How could a lone gunman have escaped without considerable help? The FBI's entry into the case seemed to confirm the presence of a conspiracy. The FBI cannot become involved in the investigation of a plain murder, no matter how important the victim is, unless it can be proved that the victim was transported across state lines or unless a conspiracy is suspected. Within a few hours after the King killing, Tennessee police had traced the rifle dropped in front of the store on Main Street in Memphis to the Aeromarine Supply Company in Birmingham, Alabama. The store clerks confirmed that the rifle had been purchased by a Harvey Lowmyer whose description was similar to that of the roomer at Mrs. Brewer's. They remembered his mentioning that he might go hunting with his brother. Because there was good reason to assume that John L. Willard and Harvey Lowmyer were the same man, and because the man calling himself Lowmyer had mentioned a brother, it was possible for the FBI to enter the case. The presence of a brother indicated the possibility of a conspiracy.

As soon as the FBI became involved in the investigation, a lid of secrecy was clamped down tightly on the case. The secrecy was necessary. Witnesses and those with pertinent information were fearful for their safety, for who knew what sinister forces would be out to get them if their identity was learned? Also, the FBI did not want the killer or conspirators to find out what they knew. The case would be pursued in the months that followed with an absence of leaks never before or since duplicated. Reporters assigned to the case were endlessly frustrated in their attempts to find out what was going on. No one, it seemed, was telling anything.

As a result, the rumors of conspiracy grew, fostered not a little by the same frustrated reporters. What was the government trying to hide? There was a precedent for such suspicion, in the handling of the John F. Kennedy assassination case. The man convicted of his murder, Lee Harvey Oswald, had in turn been murdered by Dallas businessman Jack Ruby while Oswald was actually in police custody. The subsequent report of the commission that studied the facts of the case had concluded that Oswald had acted alone, but rumors of Cuban and CIA connections had, in the opinion of many, never been satisfactorily dispelled. Charges of a government "whitewash" remained very much alive. Was there some connection between the King and Kennedy assassinations, many wondered?

Meanwhile, the search for James Earl Ray was developing into the biggest manhunt in history. There were days on which 1500 FBI agents were all working on some aspect of the case. Thousands of witnesses would be interviewed, some many times over, tens of thousands of pages of records would be examined, and eventually the governments of several countries would be involved, not to mention local authorities from Maine to California.

There were, of course, a number of clues to work on right from the beginning. Mrs. Brewer, proprietor of the boarding house at 422½ South Main Street, as well as some of her roomers, had described the tenant who had called himself John L. Willard as about 5'10", about 130 pounds, with dark hair, a receding hairline and a long, thin nose. There were fingerprints in the room in which he had stayed and a handprint on the wall of the hall bathroom, next to the tub. However, none of these prints turned out to be clear enough for identification. The contents of the overnight bag dropped with the rifle in front of a nearby store were not very helpful—hotel-size bars of soap, other toilet items, a roll of toilet tissue, shoe polish, vitamins, underwear—but two items were of some interest. One was the first section of the *Memphis Commercial Appeal*, dated April 4, 1968, carrying a headline about King and a picture of him in front of the Lorraine Motel, the number 306 clearly readable above the door. The other was a pair of pliers with the name ROMAGE HARDWARE stamped on the handle. It did not take long to locate a Romage Hardware store in Los Angeles, California, and by Saturday April 6 agents had determined that the pliers had been purchased sometime between October 1966 and April 4, 1968.

On April 11, agents located an abandoned white Mustang in Atlanta and found it was registered to an Eric S. Galt, 2608 South Highland Avenue, Birmingham. The address turned out to be a boarding house whose owner remembered Galt staying there from August to October 1967. His description of Galt led agents to believe he could be the same man who had used the names John L. Willard and Harvey Lowmyer. In the car they found a sticker showing that it had been serviced in Los Angeles in February 1968. On the same day, April 11, the laundry mark on the underwear left in the overnight bag in Memphis was traced to a laundry in Los Angeles. According to their records, the underwear belonged to an Eric S. Galt. Post office records revealed where Galt had lived while in Los Angeles. On March 17 he had checked out of the cheap hotel, giving his forwarding address as General

Delivery, Atlanta, Georgia. Clearly, Harvey Lowmyer, John L. Willard, and Eric S. Galt were the same man. But who was this man? There was no record of any of the three names in FBI or police files in the whole country. And the trail the FBI had been following seemed to end in Atlanta with the abandoned white Mustang.

FBI agents continued their search. A cocktail waitress in the Los Angeles hotel where Galt had stayed recalled that Galt had once mentioned he was taking dancing lessons. That led agents eventually to the National Dance Studio, where teachers remembered his mentioning taking bartending lessons, which led to the International School of Bartending in Los Angeles. There, at last, they found a photograph of Galt. It had been taken upon his graduation from the course and though his eyes were tight shut in the photograph a police artist was able to draw eyes in. Witnesses who had described Lowmyer and Willard identified the photograph.

Back in the South, a room which Galt had rented in Atlanta had been located. In it agents found a map of Atlanta with the locations of King's home, SCLC headquarters, and Ebenezer Baptist Church circled. And they found, at last, a clear fingerprint which, two days later, was matched with the FBI file fingerprints of James Earl Ray. After a comparison of police mug shots with the bartending school photograph, the FBI knew at last whom they were looking for: James Earl Ray, escaped convict. He was immediately placed on the FBI's "Ten Most Wanted Fugitives" list and his photograph was prominent on front pages all over North America. It was recognized in Toronto, but no trace of a James Earl Ray could be found there.

Meanwhile rumors about the King assassination and the

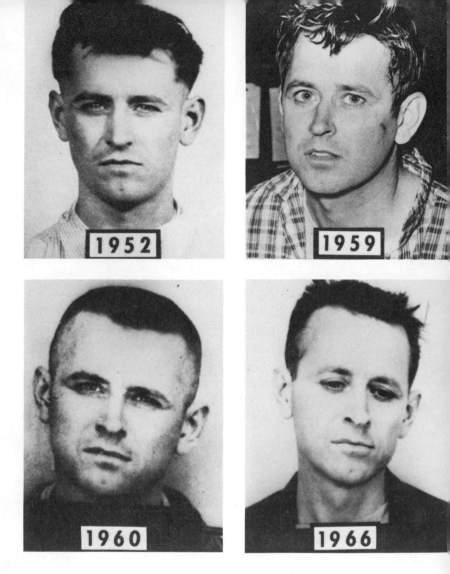

1952

1959

1960

1966

Some of the questions in the assassination case involve the physical description of the man who was seen by various persons at various key sites. As these four prison mug shots show, James Earl Ray's appearance could change remarkably. (UNITED PRESS INTERNATIONAL) person or persons behind it were rampant in the United States. Many who were convinced of a conspiracy believed that Ray was dead. Surely now that his identity was known he was too dangerous for his fellow conspirators to allow him to live. Once Ray's identity had been made public, reporters who'd been denied access to information about the case went zealously to work learning about Ray's background. Their reports of his petty criminal and small-time career did not seem to fit a man who had so far eluded the largest law enforcement network in the free world. The calls for full disclosure of the details of the investigation by the FBI became louder and more insistent.

The object of all this controversy remained quite alive and very active. He had arrived in Toronto on April 8 and had rented a room for two weeks using the name Paul Edward Bridgman. A week after that he had rented a room in another rooming house under the name Ramon George Sneyd. Thereafter, he stayed at one place during the day and the other at night. On April 16, the same day he rented the second room, he went to the Kennedy Travel Bureau and inquired about round-trip excursion tickets to London. The manager asked if he had a passport, and when Ray replied "Not yet," she kindly offered to get it for him. It would take about two weeks, she said, so Ray booked a BOAC flight to London on May 6. When the passport arrived, Ray realized his block printing on the application form had been mis-read. Instead of SNEYD, the last name was given as SNEYA. Still, it did not prevent him from taking his trip. As planned, on Monday, May 6, he flew to London, leaving behind his small flight bag in the second rooming house.

Arriving in London on May 7, Ray, still traveling as Ramon George Sneyd, immediately flew on to Lisbon, Portugal, from which city he hoped to get to Africa as a white mercenary. But he could not make any connections in the strange city whose language he did not speak. A little over a week later he was at Lisbon Airport bound for a plane back to London. Airport customs noticed the discrepancy between the names on his entry card and his passport and advised him to have it corrected. The Canadian Embassy in Lisbon issued a new passport to him with the correct name, Sneyd, but warned him to keep the "Sneya" passport because it had the stamp showing that he had entered Portugal legally. Arriving in London, Ray continued his search for a way to get to Africa as a white mercenary, although he was advised it was a poor time to do so, since there were not many mercenary forces left in Africa.

Back in the United States, although Ray's trail had gone cold in Canada, the FBI and local authorities in various areas had plenty of work to do. They were busy trying to reconstruct Ray's movements and activities from the time he escaped from prison, April 23, 1967, to the day of the assassination, April 4, 1968. Taken together, this is what the agents' reports showed:

After breaking out of prison, Ray had made his way to Illinois where, in a little town outside of Chicago, he had gotten a job as a dishwasher and saved enough money to buy a secondhand Plymouth. Then he headed for Canada, arriving in Montreal around July 13. There he signed the name Eric S. Galt to an apartment lease and two weeks later held up a store for $1700, getting away clean for a change. Within a few days he ordered a suit made for him at the English and Scotch Woolen Company. He would not be back for the suit, he told the clerk; he wanted it sent to him at 2608 Highland Avenue, Birmingham, Alabama.

He arrived in Birmingham on August 25 and stayed there until October 7, renting a room at Economy Grill and Rooms. During his stay in Birmingham, he took dancing lessons and purchased camera equipment. He also bought the white Mustang and obtained a driver's license in the name of Eric S. Galt.

On October 7 he checked out of his room in Birmingham and drove to Mexico, where he stayed about five weeks. He gave his profession as "publisher's assistant" and seems to have lived a very relaxed life, sleeping late, sunning himself on the beach, hanging around in bars. He enjoyed a close relationship with a woman named Irma and even asked her to marry him. She refused. He tried to establish a relationship with another woman named Alicia, whom he told he was smuggling marijuana and asked to help him. This relationship did not last either. A week later, Ray was on his way to Los Angeles.

In Los Angeles, still using the name Eric S. Galt, he tried to get a job, placing two ads in the *Los Angeles Times*, but his prospective employers required either police clearance or Social Security identification, neither of which Ray had for the name Eric Starvo Galt. He ran into the same problem when he answered employment ads in the newspapers. He took dancing and bartending lessons. He even went to a psychiatrist to get help in overcoming his shyness. Interestingly, he used his real name, James Earl Ray, with the psychiatrist. FBI agents theorized that Ray had expected the psychiatrist would hypnotize him and find out his real name anyway. He became friendly with a cocktail waitress named Marie and spent many evenings in the bar where she worked. On the evening of December 14, the woman introduced him to her cousin, Rita Stein, and told him Rita needed a way to get her children from her mother's home in New Orleans and bring them back to Los Angeles. Ray agreed to make the trip and it was decided that Rita's brother, Charlie, would go with him and help him drive. Ray said he had some business of his own to transact in New Orleans anyway. They left on December 17 and returned around December 21.

On March 5, 1968, Ray visited a plastic surgeon and had the tip of his nose removed. A little over a week later, on March 17, he filed a change of address card, giving his new address as General Delivery, Atlanta, Georgia. Learning of Galt's planned trip east, Marie asked him to drop off a package in New Orleans, which he did; then he drove to Selma, Alabama, where he spent the night of March 22. On March 24 he took a room at Garner's rooming house in Atlanta, the same room in which the map of Atlanta was later found. Five days later he purchased the rifle at Aeromarine Supply, exchanged it the next day, and then went to Memphis. The FBI had then traced him to the New Rebel Motel and finally, to Mrs. Brewer's rooming house.

Once he had checked into the rooming house, the FBI theorized, Ray set about lining up his target. At first he had planned to shoot from the window of his room. After the shooting, police found the curtain pulled back and draped over a dresser next to the window and a chair pulled up to the sill. Then, looking for a clearer shot, he had gone down the hall to the bathroom, where he had rested the rifle on the windowsill. The barrel had made an indentation in the weathered, soft wood. He had realized at some point, according to the FBI theory, that although he would have no trouble hitting his target from that distance because the rifle was equipped with a scope, he would have difficulty identifying his target. He was some two hundred yards away, and any short, rather stout man in a suit could be mistaken for King, which explained why he drove to the York Arms Company and purchased an inexpensive pair of binoculars. Returning to the rooming house, he waited in the bathroom until King emerged from his room. Then he took aim and fired the one fatal shot, after which he returned to his room, grabbed his flight bag, wrapped the gun in the old bedspread he carried with him and made his way down the stairs to the street. He probably had not intended to drop his bundles and had done so only because he had seen the police coming his way. He got into his Mustang and drove away, somehow eluding the police. The next day he arrived in Atlanta where he abandoned the car and headed for Canada, probably using interstate public transportation.

While some agents were piecing together this story, other agents searched for a motive for the killing and tried to ascertain whether or not Ray had confederates. They interviewed his family, men who had served in prison with him, people he had known in California. What emerged was a picture of a very complex man. He was a loner. He was insecure about his social behavior—why else take dancing and bartending lessons?—particularly around women. Although he had never been a member of the Ku Klux Klan or any White Citizens organization, he was a racist. Once he had refused an offer to be transferred to a prison honor farm because he had heard there were blacks there. He was keenly interested in Rhodesia and South Africa, where a minority of whites held power over majority black populations, and very supportive of the white governments.

He was also very much interested in money and often talked about making one "big lick" that would net him enough to retire in style. There was another possible motive that could not be discounted, not with a man like James Earl Ray, and that was ego, the desire of a habitual loser to prove that he was smarter than anyone else.

By the end of May, 1968, Ray had begun to get desperate. He still had not found a way to get to Africa as a white mercenary. Low on funds, he held up a bank on June 4. On the morning of June 8 he checked out of his hotel room and traveled to London's Heathrow Airport bound for a plane to Brussels, Belgium. The British Immigration Officer who checked his passport noticed the second passport in his billfold. While Ray was explaining the difference in last name spellings on the two passports, he was approached by a Scotland Yard detective. Four days earlier, the Royal Canadian Mounted Police had at last traced Ray to the Toronto travel bureau and connected him with the name Ramon George Sneyd. A secret, all-ports warning had been issued by Scotland Yard. On June 8, just over two months after the assassination, James Earl Ray was apprehended. Three days earlier, Senator Robert Kennedy had been fatally shot in California and had died the following morning. There seemed no end to the American tragedy.

Police and FBI agents in Los Angeles guarded Sirhan Sirhan, Kennedy's assassin, as if he were wired with dynamite and everyone in the city carried lit fuses. No one wanted a repeat performance of the Dallas fiasco in which the man who had killed John F. Kennedy had in turn been killed. But if uncommon security measures were taken with Sirhan, extraordinary precautions were taken with James Earl Ray. Sirhan Sirhan was just dynamite; Ray was pure nitroglycerine. When extradition proceedings from England were completed, he was transported in the dead of night on July 18 on a special Air Force jet from London to Memphis and from there to a specially prepared cell. Its windows were covered with quarter-inch steel plates; it was equipped with continuously burning high intensity lights. Microphones so sensitive that they could monitor breathing were installed, and television cameras recorded every movement. Memphis authorities were prepared for everything from small artillery fire to the various means by which Ray could take his own life. As long as he was in their custody he was going to be kept alive.

Ray had engaged a lawyer while still in London. He was Birmingham attorney Arthur Hanes, Sr., who was known not only as a former mayor of Birmingham but also as the attorney who had successfully defended three Ku Klux Klansmen accused of murdering a civil rights worker in March 1965. Hanes had flown to London in early July and had talked with his client, but on Saturday July 20, at Shelby County Jail, Hanes and Ray had their first substantive conference. That morning and the next two mornings Ray would tell his lawyer his story.

He had escaped from the Missouri state penitentiary not in a bread box but by scaling a prison wall, using a long window pole, he said. He had worked in the restaurant in Illinois, saved up enough to buy a used Plymouth, and headed for Montreal. There he had assumed the alias Eric Starvo Galt (he had just picked out the names at random from a sign and something he remembered reading). Also in Montreal, he had met by chance a red-haired French

Canadian sailor named Raoul who had offered him money to do some "jobs" for him. From September 1967 to April 1968, he had worked for Raoul, who had promised in return to get him identity and travel papers so he could get to a foreign country, and to give him twelve thousand dollars cash besides.

At first he had performed smuggling operations, transporting drugs, jewels, and rare coins from Canada and Mexico into the United States. Raoul had given him money whenever he needed it and told him where to go, what motels to register in, and where the two should rendezvous at various times and in various parts of the North American continent.

Early in March, Ray went on, Raoul wrote to him care of General Delivery, Los Angeles (as was the usual practice) and asked Ray to meet him in New Orleans on the twentieth of the month, informing him that they would then go to Atlanta for a while. Upon arriving in New Orleans and telephoning the number Raoul had given him, however, Ray received a message that Raoul had gone on to Birmingham. He went to Birmingham, met Raoul there, and together they drove to Atlanta, where Raoul told him they were going into gun-running—buying rifles in the United States and smuggling them into Mexico and possibly other Latin American countries. Ray was to purchase one rifle as a sample, which they would then show their first customers, who were in Memphis. Raoul showed Ray a newspaper advertisement for the Aeromarine Supply Company in Birmingham and gave him seven hundred dollars to purchase the rifle, a scope, and ammunition.

On March 29 Ray purchased a rifle at Aeromarine Supply, using the name Harvey Lowmyer, and returned to his motel room where Raoul was waiting. The Canadian told Ray he'd purchased the wrong gun and Ray went back the next day to get the right one. The first day he'd given the store clerks a story about planning to go hunting with his brother, and when he returned he explained that his brother had told him he'd gotten the wrong gun. Raoul approved the second purchase and told Ray to go to Memphis. Raoul had to go back to New Orleans for a couple of days, but he would meet Ray in Memphis soon. At 3 p.m. on April 4, Ray, using the name John L. Willard, was to check in at a rooming house at 422½ South Main Street, where the two would rendezvous.

Ray said he had dutifully gone on to Memphis and stayed at the New Rebel Motel until the afternoon of April 4, when he had located the rooming house on South Main Street and paid the landlady, Mrs. Brewer, for a week in advance. Raoul had entered Room 5B shortly after Ray's arrival, ordered Ray to park his white Mustang closer to the house and on the way to purchase a pair of infrared binoculars. He did not know what infrared binoculars were, Ray said, so he had bought a pair of ordinary binoculars at a store nearby. By then it was nearly half past five p.m. and Raoul had suggested that Ray have a beer at Jim's Grill downstairs while Raoul washed and dressed. Ray had his beer, according to his account, then went out to the car to wait for Raoul. He was standing by the car when he heard a shot. Moments later Raoul appeared, carrying something long and wrapped in the bedspread Ray usually carried with him. The red-haired man dropped the bundle in front of a shop as he passed it, then bolted for Ray's car, jumped in and covered himself with a white sheet Ray had in the back. Ray had just then seen a horde of policemen rushing out of a nearby fire station. He leaped behind the wheel of his car and took off.

About four blocks later, he had to stop for a red light. Raoul whipped the sheet from his body, opened the door, and jumped out. "See you in New Orleans," he called, but Ray never saw him again.

After that, Ray said, he'd been on his own. He'd wanted to go to New Orleans to get the identity and travel papers and the twelve thousand dollars promised him, but once he'd heard of King's assassination and connected it with the shot he'd heard he had been too afraid. He'd abandoned the Mustang in Atlanta and set off for Canada by bus—Atlanta to Cincinnati, Cincinnati to Detroit, Detroit to Canada. From Canada he had gone to London, and in London he had been apprehended.

Hanes was convinced that Ray, as well as King, had been the victim of a "giant conspiracy." In his opinion, Ray wasn't a "crazy," not a pathological "nigger hater " (and Hanes had known such men). In fact, he seemed to Hanes a very calm, self-possessed man. Hanes told the press he thought Ray was just a pawn. The prosecuting attorneys felt the same way. Assistant Attorneys General Robert K. Dwyer and James Beasley didn't know a lot about James Earl Ray, but from what little they did know they did not think he was capable of having acted alone. They were also keenly aware of the conspiracy talk, rampant across the country, and they were determined not to be dupes of some government scheme. The prosecution began its own massive investigations, looking for evidence of a conspiracy, checking and double-checking the information and witnesses already found and questioned by the FBI and local authorities. Meanwhile Ray's attorney, Arthur Hanes, was also looking for evidence of a conspiracy, although on a smaller scale; after all, the defense had only to prove a "reasonable doubt" that Ray was guilty.

In the next weeks Hanes found a number of witnesses and information which collectively seemed to provide that "reasonable doubt." There were the two men who claimed to have been in the vicinity of the bushes below the back wall of 422½ South Main Street at the time of the shooting: one reported that a man had run past him so close that he'd kicked gravel on him; the other told of seeing someone with a *white sheet* over his head running from the area. There was the hospital attendant who rode in the ambulance that took King to the hospital and who said there was not just the one huge wound in the right jaw but several small wounds below it, in the neck. There was the testimony of private investigator Renfro J. Hays whom Hanes had hired to help him. Hays had staged a re-enactment of the shooting, using goats as victims (for goats' bones and flesh most closely approximate those of humans) and although he had used the same type of gun, shot at the same distance and aimed at the same area of the body, none of the goats had suffered the same kind of wound as King had. If a bullet should cause similar damage in a human body as in a goat's body, why weren't the wounds similar?

The woman in the room next door to Ray's at 422½ South Main Street had told the police she had not seen anyone walk past her door after the shot. Now she told Hanes she had seen a stocky, gray-haired man in his fifties wearing a plaid sport shirt under a military jacket and carrying a long bundle. A man from Nashville telephoned Hanes. He'd been at the Brewer rooming house on April 4 and had met a man in the hall near the bathroom that afternoon. He was blond, stocky, late forties, wearing a white shirt and a military jacket. They were clearly the same man, Hanes thought excitedly. The man claimed to have been with the stocky blond stranger when he had fired the shot. He'd been too frightened to come forward before.

Hanes was certain he could establish reasonable doubt until he examined the state's physical evidence, which, in Tennessee, a defense attorney is allowed to do. When he finished he was worried. The state had a solid case against Ray. His witnesses and the results of Hay's goat experiments suddenly seemed inadequate when set against the state's treasure trove of evidence and three hundred witnesses. He knew the jury, like the rest of the country, would want to believe the conspiracy theory, but he couldn't seem to get enough solid information from Ray to put forth the theory in court. The trial was set for Tuesday November 12, and he was beginning to be exasperated with Ray, who didn't seem to be telling him the whole story. Ray had lately talked about taking the stand in his own defense. Hanes felt that would be disastrous. He became more and more worried about the trial. Perhaps, he suggested, Ray should consider pleading guilty or making some sort of deal with the state.

Ray dismissed Hanes as his lawyer and hired Percy Foreman, an attorney famous for successfully defending accused murderers. Foreman's fees were high, but Ray made the same arrangements with him as he had with Hanes: author William Bradford Huie had offered Ray thirty thousand dollars for his exclusive story, and Ray would pay Foreman from that money. Because of the last-minute change and Foreman's need for time to prepare his case, the trial was postponed until March 1969.

By mid-December, Foreman had concluded it would be a miracle if he were ready with his case by March. He, too, had examined the state's physical evidence and realized he could not disprove it. He would have to rely on reasonable doubt. But evidence pointing to reasonable doubt was almost nonexistent. The witnesses Hanes had come up with now either denied their stories or did not want to testify. He had the goat experiments but little else. Interviewing Ray, he was experiencing the same frustration Hanes had felt. He caught him in lies, in altered stories; he sensed his client wasn't telling him everything. At last he also suggested that Ray plead guilty. Initially Ray was completely against it.

By the end of December, Foreman was convinced that a guilty plea was the best tactic and Ray had begun to listen. Previously, Ray had believed that no southern jury would convict him. But Foreman reminded him that the South had become concerned with its racist image. Here and there, all-white juries were beginning to convict white people accused of crimes against blacks and to acquit black people accused of crimes. A jury in Ray's trial might just convict him to prove that Tennessee wasn't racist, Foreman argued. Foreman had informed the state's attorneys of the possible change in plea and they in turn had contacted Coretta King's personal attorney to find out how the King family would react. The Kings, they were told, would approve the plea. Although they had some doubts that Ray had acted alone, they realized that evidence of a conspiracy would probably not come out in the trial anyway.

About two weeks before the trial, Foreman obtained a signed statement from Ray in which he agreed to plead guilty. In doing so, he was accepting a ninety-nine-year prison sentence. But, Foreman explained, if he pleaded not guilty and was convicted, he faced the death sentence. Two days before the trial Ray wanted to retract his statement. Foreman persuaded him not to.

On Monday March 10, 1969—coincidentally Ray's forty-first birthday—a special hearing was called by Judge W. Preston Battle. James Earl Ray pleaded guilty. Judge Battle questioned him over and over again to make sure, for the record, that Ray understood all the ramifications of his decision: that he could not later submit a motion for a new trial, or petition any higher court on appeal; that there was no possibility of parole; and that he would not later claim to have been coerced into pleading guilty. To each question but one Ray answered unhesitatingly: yes, he understood this point and this point and this point; no, he had not been coerced. Only when Battle asked, "Are you pleading guilty of murder in the first degree in this case because you killed Dr. Martin Luther King under such circumstances that it would make you legally guilty of murder in the first degree under the law as explained to you by your lawyers?" did Ray seem to hedge. "Yes, legally, yes," he answered.

The courtroom buzzed after the exchange was completed. Both prosecuting attorneys and defense attorney, as well as Judge Battle, realized the spectators were muttering "cover-up," "whitewash." State Attorney General Philip Canale felt it was his duty to address the subject of conspiracy. He described the scope of the investigation and stated that no evidence of conspiracy had been found, that the only proof they had indicated that Ray had acted alone.

Then Foreman rose. He also had come to the conclusion that there was no conspiracy, although it had taken him a month to convince himself that the Attorney General of the United States, Ramsey Clark, and J. Edgar Hoover of the FBI were stating a fact when they said that Ray had acted alone.

When he finished speaking, Foreman turned to take his seat. Suddenly Ray stood up. Now, *he* wanted to say something.

"The only thing I have to say is, I don't exactly accept the theories of Mr. Clark," he began.

The judge wanted to know what he meant.

"I mean Mr. Canale, Mr. Clark, and Mr. J. Edgar Hoover," he explained. "I mean on the conspiracy thing. I don't want to add something onto it that I haven't agreed to in the past."

Did he want to change any of his answers to the questions he had been asked earlier? Judge Battle wanted to know. No, Ray didn't.

The trial proceeded with the necessary formalities. The jury was chosen; the prosecution made a brief presentation of its case, questioning expert witnesses, summarizing its proof. The defense, of course, did not present any arguments. The case went to the jury, which never left the room. The defendant had pleaded guilty and thus the twelve jurors had no real decision-making responsibility. James Earl Ray stood to hear the sentence to which he had agreed—ninety-nine years in the state penitentiary.

The entire trial had taken less than three hours, but it had been long enough to leave a bad taste in the mouth of everyone connected with it, not to mention the rest of the American public.

Chapter 7
Unanswered
Questions

The vehemence of the angry public reaction surprised even those who thought they had fully prepared themselves for it. State Attorney General Canale, the two other prosecuting attorneys, Dwyer and Beasley, and Judge Battle were vilified in the press, and charges of conspiracy were loud and specific. The American public felt cheated, hoodwinked. At least Ray should have been allowed to take his chances. He must have been coerced into pleading guilty so the government could keep the lid on the conspiracy. For many, there could no longer be any doubt that a cover-up had taken place. The reaction was in some ways comparable to that which occurred some years later when President Gerald Ford pardoned former President Richard Nixon. Many Americans felt that justice should have been allowed to take its course. They felt cheated. Reaction to the Ray plea and trial was ten times as ferocious and almost universal. *No one* was satisfied, least of all the principals in the matter.

James Earl Ray had not even reached the state penitentiary in Nashville when he changed his mind. He'd been railroaded by his lawyer, he charged. He was *not* guilty; he had *not* killed King. He wrote to Judge Battle demanding a post-conviction hearing. Battle did not respond but left for a brief and sorely needed vacation. Upon his return he found another letter from Ray. The convicted man intended to ask for a reversal of his sentence and he wanted new attorneys to represent him. Judge W. Preston Battle had a heart attack. When he was found, his head was resting on Ray's letter on top of his desk. Ray then cited a Tennessee law under which if a judge died while a request for a new trial was under his consideration the request must be granted. (Ray was a fairly competent "jailhouse lawyer.") But Battle's successor ruled against Ray, citing the exhaustive round of questioning the deceased judge had gone through with Ray when he entered his guilty plea in court.

Ray's new attorneys were J. B. Stoner, lawyer for the anti-black National States Rights party, Richard J. Ryan, a campaign manager for George Wallace in the Memphis area, and Chattanooga lawyer Robert W. Hill. They began to push for a new trial for Ray on the ground that King's death had been arranged by the FBI and that Ray had been used like a pawn in a chess game.

Ray, meanwhile, had changed his story. He told Hill, who had prime responsibility for questioning him, that he had not been standing outside the rooming house when the shot was fired but in fact had been several blocks away. He had intended to wait for Raoul outside, but he had noticed one of the Mustang's tires had a slow leak and so he had driven to a service station to have it fixed. Driving back to South Main Street, he said, he saw a police car parked at an intersection stopping traffic, and he had immediately headed south, intending to call Raoul later to find out what had happened. He had not learned of King's shooting until he had gotten miles into Mississippi. Hearing that the police were looking for a white Mustang, he had driven to Atlanta and abandoned the car there. When Hill asked Ray why he had changed his story, particularly that crucial part of it, Ray cited the book William Bradford Huie was writing. He had thought that saying he was on the scene at the time of the murder made better copy and would sell more books.

Hill had removed himself from the case by the spring of 1970. He was replaced by Bernard Fensterwald, Jr., executive director of the Committee to Investigate Assassinations, a non-profit organization made up of people who suspected that the King and Kennedy murders might be related. Fensterwald, Stoner, and Ryan would take Ray's case to the Memphis Criminal Court, the State Court of Criminal Appeals, and the State Supreme Court, but to no avail. By the spring of 1971 the only avenues left to them were in the federal court system, but Ray was as determined as ever to secure a new trial.

The man's persistent denial of his guilt disturbed some in the Justice Department, and in 1971 the Civil Rights Division, which had assumed primary responsibility for investigating the killing almost from the moment that it had occurred, assigned a group of its lawyers to reread and reexamine the material and reports from the FBI's initial investigation. The purpose of the new inquiry was to determine whether there were enough unanswered questions to warrant reopening the case. In addition to examining the FBI's material, the lawyers did some detective work of their own and reinterviewed some of the major witnesses and others connected with the case whose stories seemed to raise questions. But they were unable to clear up the matter. The unanswered questions remained unanswered, and yet they did not seem, even collectively, to warrant a new, full-scale inquiry.

Meanwhile the civil rights movement, identified so closely with the last thirteen years of King's life, had abated considerably, as it was beginning to do even before the assassination. Federal civil rights legislation assured a gradual but steady change in the social structure of the South, where desegregation of nearly all facilities except schools proceeded and slowly became accepted. The national racial spotlight shifted away from the South to California and to northern cities where the Black Panthers enjoyed a brief and violent career. The loudest and most often heard black voices now were those of the young militants who shunned integration and opposed emulation of white standards. "Black is beautiful" became a popular slogan; many blacks, young and not so young, adopted "natural" hair styles, African-style dress, and even African names. Colleges and universities had, beginning in the middle 1960's, made efforts to increase their black enrollment. By the late 1960's the black students were demanding black studies programs and all-black dormitories.

The Southern Christian Leadership Conference continued to function, led by King's chief aide, the Reverend Ralph David Abernathy, but nationally its voice was weak. The Poor People's March on Washington, for which King had held such high hopes, had been staged despite the assassination and had been very well attended. But it had not led to any national poor people's movement. Had King lived, he might have been able to inspire such a movement, but he was dead and so was the vitality of the SCLC. Coretta King became much more active after her husband's death, for she felt a responsibility to continue his mission. She traveled extensively, in the United States as well as abroad, and gradually became respected not just as the widow of a slain martyr but as a strong, committed, and forward-looking woman in her own right. She did not seek renown for herself, however. "I am acting in the name of Dr. Martin Luther King, Jr.," she would say. She was the only King family member who could. The Reverend King, Sr., was too old to manage the grueling life of a public figure, and sadly, A. D. King was not around. Sixteen months after the assassination, A. D. had drowned in a bizarre swimming accident, adding another tragic chapter to the King family story. Coretta King, however, could not replace her husband as a national black leader. No one could. Black leadership splintered, and with it went whatever unity black Americans had enjoyed.

By 1974 the American black community had quieted, as had the young white radicals. After nearly a decade of social upheaval the country as a whole was exhausted. The end of U. S. involvement in Vietnam deprived the New Left of its major rallying issue. College campuses were calm; the cities were quiet. As the economic recession set in and worsened, Americans turned their attention to their own livelihood and survival and became less interested in causes.

James Earl Ray doggedly pursued his case, causing the Justice Department to reopen the investigation once again. The voluminous FBI files were reread and the evidence reexamined, and this time, too, questions remained for which there seemed no answers. However, the lawyers reviewing the case were more certain than those who had done so in 1971 that Ray "probably" had acted alone. But Ray persisted in his claim to innocence, and that year his lawyers took his case to the U. S. Sixth Circuit Court of Appeals, charging that Ray had been unconstitutionally coerced by Foreman into pleading guilty. It was in that court that the first break in the long effort came, for an evidentiary hearing was held in February 1975. Had the judge ruled in Ray's favor, a new trial would have been possible. But after hearing ten days of arguments, the judge ruled against him. Once more Ray's efforts for a new trial were stalled. However, outside and apparently unrelated events were occurring that would generate new interest in the King assassination and in the case of James Earl Ray.

Among the major aspects of the Watergate break-in and cover-up scandal was the involvement of U. S. intelligence agencies. One of the burglars was a former Central Intelligence Agency (CIA) man, and the others also had CIA connections. When the break-in was discovered, the FBI immediately launched an investigation, but President Nixon's aides ordered the agency to "soft-pedal" their inquiry, explaining that it might expose CIA operations and thus threaten national security. The FBI, supposedly an agency independent of the Chief Executive, had complied with the order. This information was later revealed during the congressional Watergate hearings, and the country was as shocked to learn about the complicity and shady dealings of its intelligence agencies as it was about the President's abuse of power. This is not to say that there had been no suspicions about these agencies before Watergate. Radicals on both the left and right of the political spectrum had frequently charged that the FBI and CIA were engaged in spying operations against American citizens and were, in effect, equivalent to the secret police of communist countries. But probably the majority of Americans had preferred to believe that the agencies were not overstepping their bounds. After Watergate, this belief was shattered. The United States, so lately divided by conflict between blacks and whites and between pro-war and anti-war forces, was once more in turmoil, embroiled in a crisis of confidence in the very agencies and persons on whom they were supposed ultimately to rely for their safety and well-being.

In the fall of 1975 the Senate Intelligence Committee began an extensive inquiry into the activities of the CIA and FBI, the first such inquiry in the history of either organization. The FBI was formed in 1908 as a special domestic detective force in the Department of Justice. The CIA was established in 1947 as a new and independent agency charged with gathering information on the purposes and capabilities of other countries. Both organizations were begun only after special congressional hearings to establish whether or not there was a need for them. In the hearings on each, some witnesses and congressmen had expressed fears that the proposed organizations might abuse their powers and infringe on the rights of ordinary citizens. The Senate Intelligence Committee hearings in 1975 revealed that these fears had been well founded.

What the members of the committee learned was chilling: the "unalienable rights" spelled out in the Declaration of Independence seemed, on the contrary, to be quite *alienable*. Among the committee's findings on questionable and/or illegal activities on the part of the FBI was incontrovertible evidence that the agency had harassed and spied on Martin Luther King, Jr., with a vengeance for the last six years of his life, and that J. Edgar Hoover had engaged in what amounted to a "personal vendetta" against King.

It had all started, seemingly, when King had criticized Hoover for assigning racially biased agents to southern field offices responsible for investigating the murders of civil rights workers—criticism that had probably prompted Hoover to label King "the most notorious liar in the country" in November 1964. But there was also considerable evidence that Hoover himself was a racist; all the time he was director of the FBI the Bureau had no black agents because he did not want them. In 1963 Hoover had approached the Justice Department with a request to subject King to electronic surveillance because there was evidence of communist influence within King's inner circle. Then Attorney General Robert F. Kennedy had granted permission for the installation of three wiretaps for a limited period of time. His brother, the President, had taken a political risk by supporting King and could have been severely embarrassed had the Bureau's suspicions of communist influence in the SCLC proved well founded. But the Bureau had far exceeded the authority it had been granted. It had tapped the telephones in King's house in Atlanta from 1963 to 1965 and those in his Atlanta office from 1963 to 1966. It had installed sixteen bugging microphones in hotels and motels where he stayed while traveling. A special group of FBI investigators had been detailed to gather evidence damaging to King's character; its code name was "Zorro."

Nineteen sixty-four seems to have been the most active

year for the FBI campaign against King. After *Time* Magazine had selected him as its "Man of the Year" in January, the Bureau decided to discredit King so it could promote a more moderate black leader, and when it was announced that King had been awarded the Nobel Prize for Peace the FBI acted. Thirty-four days before King was to accept the prize he received an anonymous letter accompanied by a tape (although the contents of the tape have never been disclosed, it presumably had to do with embarrassing extramarital activities on King's part). The letter referred to the tape and said in part: "King, there is only one thing left for you to do. You know what it is. You have just 34 days in which to do it. (This exact number has been selected for a specific reason.) It has definite practical significance. You are done. There is no way out."

King had interpreted the letter and its accompanying evidence as urging him to commit suicide. This implication is not clear. More clear is the FBI's intent to shame King into giving up his prize or resigning as chairman of the SCLC or both. A copy of the tape was sent to Coretta King. The FBI would have been very pleased, of course, if she had divorced her husband, an action which would have discredited King considerably. But nothing had happened. Mrs. King had not divorced her husband. King had not committed suicide, nor had he refused to accept the Nobel Prize for Peace, nor had he resigned his chairmanship of the SCLC. In fact, he apparently had not changed his life-style one jot, which says something for the man's courage.

The FBI seems to have hounded King right up to his death. An internal Bureau memo in March 1968 suggested that the agency use friendly media contacts to say that

King was a hypocrite for going to Memphis to lead the sanitationmen's strike while he himself was staying at a white-owned Holiday Inn. (King had stayed at the motel during his first visit to Memphis, when the march in which he participated became violent.) Two local news stories had subsequently mentioned the fact.

Memos describing ways to "take King off his pedestal" and "reduce his influence" came to light, as well as documentation of attempts to persuade various universities to withdraw honorary degrees that they planned to award to King. And after King's assassination, when a proposal reached Congress to have his birthday declared a national holiday, the FBI scheduled briefings on King's character for some legislators. Indeed, it all did seem to add up to a vendetta against King, a vendetta whose prime backer had been FBI Director J. Edgar Hoover. Its personal nature was indicated by other memos in FBI files—field reports that King and the SCLC posed no threats to national security—and by testimony that Hoover had disregarded and rejected those reports, even sometimes ordering that they be rewritten to conform more closely to his opinion.

Hoover was not around to be embarrassed by these revelations, for he had died in May 1972. He had wielded extraordinary power, and it is unlikely that the illicit activities of the FBI would have come to light during his lifetime.

The findings and reports of the Senate Intelligence Committee had a profound impact on many Americans. Most of the repercussions were of a general nature—recognition of the distance the intelligence agencies had gone beyond the law and their defined activities, and realization that some sort of overseeing apparatus was necessary to ensure that they would never again overstep their authority to such an extent. There were some specific areas of impact as well, and one of these areas was the assassination of Martin Luther King, Jr., and the conviction of James Earl Ray.

The FBI had clearly harassed and tried to discredit Dr. King. Had the Bureau also been somehow responsible for or implicated in his death? The major part of the investigation into King's assassination had been conducted by the FBI—indeed, by the very "Zorro" force previously selected to destroy his reputation! Had the Bureau deliberately hidden evidence of a conspiracy? Had it even initiated a full-scale cover-up? In the light of the Senate Committee's revelations, James Earl Ray's insistence that he had been framed and railroaded into pleading guilty seemed to take on increased credibility. Late in November, Reverend Ralph David Abernathy, comedian Dick Gregory, and Georgia state legislator Hosea Williams called for a reopening of the inquiry into King's death and Coretta King stated that she believed the conspiracy theory. "I don't have the facts," she told reporters, "but at this stage I say it appears there was a conspiracy in the death of my husband."

A national poll taken by CBS showed that eighty percent of those questioned thought others were involved with James Earl Ray in the King slaying. Another poll, conducted by the Harris organization, showed that sixty percent felt he had not acted alone. Once again the unanswered questions in the case loomed large in the public mind and seemed to demand answers. In the late fall of 1975 the *New York Times* assigned a team of reporters to investigate the case with a view toward establishing whether the FBI had been involved in the killing and whether any conspiracy was indicated. The team worked six weeks; although the reporters did not have access to Ray or to certain FBI and Justice Department files, they did interview many of the major witnesses and other principals in the case. They could find no evidence either of a conspiracy or of suspicious FBI activity.

A free-lance investigative reporter from Tennessee named George McMillan had set out in 1969 to do a psychological portrait of Ray. He had spent hours interviewing members of Ray's family and, gradually gaining their confidence, had learned much that had not been previously known about the man who had been convicted of killing King. McMillan became convinced that Ray was perfectly capable of planning and implementing the assassination all by himself. On the other hand, a reporter named Jim Bishop, who had published a book about King and his assassination in 1971 in which he had indicated that Ray had acted alone, now believed differently. "I am convinced that James Earl Ray stood in a bathtub and murdered King," he wrote in a syndicated column in 1976. "A man who could not successfully engineer a simple robbery would not shoot someone for nothing. He was hired."

In Atlanta, Public Safety Commissioner A. Reginald Eaves had assigned four detectives to investigate allegations of a conspiracy in July 1975. The impetus for the investigation came from the statement of a Robert Byron Watson who said that a week before the assassination he had overheard two men in the Atlanta business where he worked discussing killing Dr. King. One of the men, Watson said, had told the other that he was going to kill King and frame someone else for it. Watson's information had been submitted to Eaves in June 1975. Eaves was not aware that the same information had been given the FBI back in April 1971 and that the Bureau had determined Watson's story was pure fabrication. Nevertheless, the Justice Department decided to reinterview Watson. The Department also decided to re-evaluate the story of a Clifford H. Andrews of Toronto, Canada, who said he had been part of a conspiracy to kill Dr. King, for which he had been promised but had never received $200,000.

Watson was a convicted drug dealer who had spent two years in prison, from 1972 to 1974, and had been convicted again in May 1975. Andrews was a convicted confidence man. After extensive investigations into the two men's stories, the Civil Rights Division of the Justice Department concluded that the two men were lying. Even Ray's lawyer, Bernard Fensterwald, agreed in an interview in late 1975 that both men appeared to be without credibility.

Then a third assertion came to light, one that involved a group of visitors to an Atlanta jail who were supposedly overheard trying to recruit inmates in a plan to kill King six months before the assassination. Such stories had been rampant ever since King's death. The FBI or other branches of the Justice Department claimed to have painstakingly checked out each of these stories and proven each to be false. Yet, in the fall of 1975 the Justice Department began yet another full-scale review of the FBI evidence.

Taking advantage of the swing of the public spotlight back to Ray, he and James H. Lesar, another attorney who had taken up Ray's cause, asked for another hearing in the Sixth Circuit Court of Appeals. This court had been somewhat sympathetic to him two years earlier—had done more than other courts in agreeing to an evidentiary hearing—and in light of the disclosures about the FBI Lesar hoped to win a ruling for a new trial by appealing the earlier unfavorable ruling. Once again, the allegation was that Percy Foreman's actions had violated Ray's right to responsible counsel. Lesar labeled Ray's guilty plea as only a "technical" plea of guilty, made because he was afraid Foreman was going to throw the trial.

Meanwhile, lawyers in the Civil Rights Division of the Justice Department completed a five-month investigation in April 1976 and recommended an expanded investigation, which Attorney General Edward H. Levi then ordered conducted by the Justice Department's new office of professional responsibility. Levi wanted conclusive answers to the unanswered questions surrounding the King assassination and the Ray case. Another new lawyer of Ray's, Robert N. Livingston, scoffed at the investigation, calling it "another cover-up." A number of other people, among them the Reverend Ralph David Abernathy, expressed some agreement with Livingston, stating that they did not think the truth would ever be known as long as the investigation was kept inside the Justice Department. How, they asked, could an impartial investigation be conducted by the very department of which the FBI was a part? Abernathy called for a "special committee of distinguished American citizens who owe no allegiance to anyone" to review the full FBI record. Yet, it was doubtful that even the findings of such a commission would be accepted by everyone. The Warren Commission itself, chaired by the late Chief Justice Earl Warren, which had been formed of such distinguished American citizens to look into the assassination of President Kennedy, had been criticized by many and its own report called a cover-up.

On May 10 a three-judge panel of the U. S. Sixth Circuit Court of Appeals ruled unanimously that James Earl Ray could not repudiate his confession. Ray had alleged that his guilty plea had not been voluntary. The judges disagreed. "The plea was entered voluntarily and knowingly," they said. Ray had contended he did not have effective lawyers in Foreman and Hanes, who were more interested in the money that would get than in defending their client. The judges said they disapproved of the arrangement Ray had made with author William Bradford Huie but that it "does not necessarily mean that Ray was denied effective assistance of counsel." Thus, Ray would not get a new trial.

Ray dismissed his chief counsel, Bernard Fensterwald. He would get another lawyer, and another, and another, if necessary, until he found one who could win his case for him. And now that his appeal had been rejected by the Circuit Court of Appeals the way had been paved for him to take his case to the highest court in the land, the United States Supreme Court, possibly as early as spring 1977.

Meanwhile, James Earl Ray waited. Released at his own request from his solitary cell in the prison's maximum security unit in August 1975, he had been placed in a small, dark cell in a regular cell block and had even been given a cell mate. He spent much of his time poring over lawbooks, looking for new angles in his case, obscure precedents, anything to further his cause. In April 1976 a reporter asked him whether it was worth it: the long court struggle, the possibility, if he was granted a new trial, of conviction anyway. Ray showed a trace of a smile when he answered, "You've never been in prison, have you? That's all I think I need to say."

Chapter 8
The Case
Is Still Open

Those persons who are actively interested in the James
Earl Ray case can be divided into two main groups, who
here shall be called the conspiracy backers and the Ray-
alone people. The conspiracy backers differ among themselves regarding who set up the King killing and gave Ray
his orders. Some, like reporter Jim Bishop, think it was a
group of wealthy Birmingham racists. Others, like *Chicago
Daily News* reporter Carl T. Rowan, think it was American anti-communists who were convinced by J. Edgar
Hoover that King was helping the Soviet Union. Still
others, like writer Joachim Joesten, an American living in
Germany who has written a book called *The James Earl
Ray Hoax*, believe Ray was a dupe in a CIA plot with
links to the assassination of President John F. Kennedy.
The King assassination, according to Joesten, was meant
to "strike fear in the hearts of black people and deprive
them of effective leadership." The Ray-alone people also
differ among themselves. Regarding Ray's motive, some
think he was a vicious racist. Others believe he expected

eventually to receive a reward for killing King, although he did not know from whom. Still others believe he was a lifelong loser who wanted fame above money, like the two-bit criminals who confess to major crimes that they have not committed in order to get attention. The majority of the Ray-alone people think he was motivated by a combination of racism, greed, and desire for attention.

There are several major aspects of the case on which the two groups disagree. One of them is motive. The conspiracy theorists point to testimony from those who knew Ray that while he might be a racist he was not fanatical about it. They also point to the fact that after his escape from prison he worked in an Illinois restaurant under a black supervisor and yet was a good worker and received successive raises. His only real motive would have been money, and if he had acted in expectation of financial reward then there must have been someone or some group that had offered him money to kill King.

The Ray-alone people point to other testimony from those who knew Ray that he was an extreme racist. Author George McMillan learned from Jerry Ray, James's brother, that after his escape from prison James had confided that he planned to kill King. He believed that Ray had received no offers of money in return for killing King, that at first he thought he would be rewarded after he had done the job—given money by grateful enemies of the black leader. Later, the matter of money declined in importance as Ray contemplated the importance the killer of King would enjoy in the eyes of the world—the publicity he would receive. All his life Ray had had big plans, grandiose schemes. This characteristic is not uncommon among petty criminals, lifelong losers, who will risk almost anything for attention even if it is criminal notoriety.

When did Ray know about or begin to plan the assassination? The conspiracy backers fall into two categories on this question. Some believe that Ray was merely a pawn and that it is quite possible he is telling the truth when he says he knew nothing of the assassination until after it happened. Some believe he may have known about it much earlier, perhaps as far back as his California period, November 1967–March 1968. Thus they are willing to accept some of the arguments of those who believe Ray acted alone, especially in light of the rather suspicious nature of some of his activities in California. However, the conspiracy backers claim that his activities were directed by others, not planned by Ray himself.

The Ray-alone people point to the new information that author George McMillan has received from Jerry Ray. According to Jerry Ray, James met his brothers Jack and Jerry in Chicago's Atlantic Hotel on April 24, 1967, the day after he escaped from prison. Jerry recalled that they were talking about Ray's money when suddenly he said, "I'm gonna kill that nigger King. That's something that's been on my mind. That's something I've been working on." Both brothers, according to Jerry, told James in no uncertain terms that if he meant what he said he would have no help from them.

The Ray-alone people then point to Ray's ordering a woolen suit in Montreal in August and having it sent to Birmingham, Alabama, where he stayed from August to October, 1967. Could he have decided to kill King then? If so, why did he not go through with it? Whatever the reason, they feel certain that by January 1968 he had definitely embarked on a specific plan, for he began to behave as if he might soon be sought by the FBI. In that month he took out an ad in the Los Angeles *Free Press* expressing his wish to meet females and offering to exchange photographs. Within the next couple of weeks he answered other ads, sending altogether some twelve Polaroid profile photographs of himself. Then, on March 5, he went to a plastic surgeon and had the tip of his long nose removed. Why, ask those who believe Ray acted alone, did the man suddenly make such an effort to get photographs of himself into the hands of a dozen girls and then have his most prominent facial feature altered unless he expected to be the subject of a nationwide search?

On March 17 Ray went to the post office in Los Angeles and filed a change-of-address card, giving his new address as General Delivery, Atlanta, Georgia. On March 24 he took a room in Garner's rooming house in Atlanta, where he circled on a map of the city the places where King frequently could be found.

Certainly, the Ray-alone people say, he could have been directed to do all this. But since no one has been identified as his boss, he must have done it alone.

What about the mysterious Raoul? Ray claims that they met by chance in a Montreal bar and that from then until the day of the assassination nearly everything he did was on Raoul's instructions. Further, Ray contended that it was Raoul who had shot King, for Raoul was on the second floor of the rooming house when the shot was fired and had come running out, carrying the gun, a few moments later. Ray described Raoul as a Latin-looking man with red hair, a seaman. The conspiracy backers believe there must have been a "Raoul" acting as a go-between, channeling orders and funds from his employers to Ray.

One of Ray's succession of lawyers, Bernard Fensterwald, had once thought he could prove Raoul's existence and even connect him with the Kennedy assassination in Dallas. He had obtained a photograph taken in Dallas half an hour after the murder, showing two men crossing the street with an FBI agent. Both men had been questioned by the FBI and later released, but Fensterwald thought it interesting that one of the men was slender and curly-haired, wearing a suit of French cut and identified as a French Canadian. Fensterwald also had a snapshot of a man called "Skinny Ralph" who, the lawyer had been told, was an American soldier of fortune trained to carry out invasions and assassinations. Fensterwald thought one of the two men in the first photograph might be this "Skinny Ralph." However, he was unable to make that connection.

There is the matter of the underwear. In the flight bag found with the rifle in front of the store on South Main Street in Memphis were found two pieces of underclothing, a T-shirt and a pair of shorts. The T-shirt was size 42-44, the shorts size 34. James Earl Ray probably could not have worn those shorts, even if he liked to wear them tight. The laundry mark on the shorts has been traced to a laundry in Los Angeles whose records show the mark belonged to an Eric S. Galt. But, say the conspiracy backers, Ray could have had someone else's laundry done along with his.

Those who believe Ray acted alone point out that Ray has never been able to make Raoul sound completely believable. Foreman reported being frustrated in his attempts to elicit information about Raoul from Ray. Though his client could give the names of numerous public places in which he had met Raoul, he could not give either the name or the description of anyone who might have remembered seeing them together. Ray has an excellent, even a remarkable, visual memory. Why couldn't he describe even a waitress or a bartender at one of those places? Ray had stated that he'd had a beer at Jim's Grill, downstairs from the rooming house on Main Street in Memphis, while waiting for Raoul. Yet, he was unable to describe the interior of the place to his first lawyer, Arthur Hanes. Later, questioned by Foreman, he described it perfectly. In the meantime, however, Hanes had described the interior of the grill to author William Bradford Huie, who made it a practice to show Ray what he was writing. Ray's description of the grill, Huie pointed out to Foreman, was almost word for word that of Arthur Hanes.

Finally, no one in the rooming house has ever mentioned seeing anyone who looked anything like Ray's description of Raoul on the day of the assassination.

How did Ray manage to support himself from April 23, 1967, when he escaped from the Missouri State Penitentiary, until June 8, 1968, when he was captured at Heathrow Airport in London? Between the time he escaped from prison and the day of the assassination he bought two cars, a green Plymouth and a white Mustang, and an expensive gun and photographic equipment, spent time in Montreal, Mexico and California, took dancing lessons and a course in bartending, began a mail-order course in locksmithing. From the time of the assassination to the time of his arrest he was in Toronto, London, and Lisbon. Where did he get the money?

Soon after his arrest, Ray supplied to Hanes an accounting of his finances from the day of his prison escape to the day he arrived in Canada after the assassination:

Left prison with $275.
　　Saved at restaurant (Winnetka) $245 Total: $520.00
After arriving in Canada first time and paying two

months rent in Montreal (first and last month), I had
approximately $90. Holdup of $1,700 gave me   1,790.00
    Spent in Canada—$1,000   790.00
    Received from Raoul in Detroit $750   1,540.00
    Received from Raoul in Birmingham $3,000 4,540.00
    Car and photo equipment cost $2,500   2,040.00
    Spent in Birmingham, $1,000   1,040.00
    Received from Raoul in Mexico $2,000   3,040.00
    Spent in Mexico, $700   2,340.00
    Received from Raoul in New Orleans $500 2,840.00
    Spent in California, $1,900   940.00
  Left California with $940
    Received from Raoul in Birmingham,
      to buy gun, $700   1,640.00
    Spent for gun, $500   1,140.00
  Arrived in Canada with $1,140.

What money I spent travelling I counted as money I
spent in the city I had just left, or was going to. *

He did not supply a financial record for the time he
spent in Canada, London, and Lisbon. He had not seen
nor heard from Raoul since the day of the assassination,
he said, and, short of funds in London, had robbed a bank
of one hundred pounds, or about $240.00.

Those who favor the conspiracy theory point to Ray's
detailed financial account and ask how he could have
gotten the money he received if not from the mysterious
Raoul or some other financial backer.

Those who believe Ray acted alone point out that

* From *An American Death* by Gerold Frank. Copyright © 1972 by
Gerold Frank. Reprinted by permission of Doubleday & Company,
Inc.

fellow prison inmates recall Ray as an enterprising jail-house businessman who dealt in drugs, prison food supplies and other commodities. Author George McMillan found two convicts who had served time with Ray at Jefferson City Prison who described how he stole eggs from the prison kitchen and sold them to fellow inmates for $1 a dozen, and made deals with prison guards to obtain drugs for him, which he would sell at a profit. The guard, or guards, with whom Ray dealt would take a percentage of the money and mail the rest to Ray's brother, Jerry, who would keep it for him. Altogether, according to McMillan, Ray had sent out from prison some $6,500. Soon after his escape from prison, Ray had met his brothers, Jack and Jerry, in a hotel in Chicago, where he had been given $4,700. About $1,500 had been kept by Jerry for Ray's use at a later date.

Ray admits to committing two robberies during the time in question, one in Montreal and one in London, which netted him close to $2000. Some people who feel that Ray acted alone theorize that he may also have committed small robberies—filling stations, neighborhood grocery stores—from time to time for ready cash. The FBI investigated all major reported and unsolved robberies in the areas where Ray was reported to have been and could not connect him with any of them. However, small holdups in which less than $500 is stolen are not recorded in FBI files. Those who believe Ray acted alone think that he could have gotten along even without committing any (or many) small holdups, that he could have done all he did on the money he admits to having stolen or earned himself plus that which his brother, Jerry, told McMillan that he gave Ray. After all, the total sum Raoul had supposedly given him was only $7,000. Ray himself had saved $6,500, which his brother Jerry had given him when he needed it.

Ray appears to have lived very frugally. He stayed in cheap, fleabag hotels and rooming houses (Mrs. Brewer's rooms at 422½ South Main Street in Memphis cost $10 a week). He collected hotel soap and carried his own bathroom tissue. He ate very inexpensively. When the white Mustang was found in Atlanta it was filled with crackers and canned soup. In the room at Garner's rooming house in Atlanta where he stayed toward the end of March 1968, FBI agents found an electric cup water heater, a bottle of salad dressing, and a plastic package of lima beans. He had gone from Toronto to London on the cheapest excursion ticket, and when he was captured in London he was carrying a newspaper advertisement for inexpensive airline rates to Africa. Certainly he had spent money on cars, photography equipment, the gun, and his various lessons, but living so penuriously he would have had the money to spend.

The conspiracy backers question Ray's ability to have secured by himself aliases that were the names of three living men whose descriptions and ages were so similar to his own, as well as new birth certificates and a passport. The Ray alone people point out that Ray has admitted to taking by himself the alias Eric Starvo Galt, although he lied about the manner in which he obtained it. He said he'd chosen the name from signs and things he remembered. But there was a real Eric S. Galt in Toronto, a businessman named Eric St. Vincent Galt, who matched Ray's general description. The difference in the middle names? Easily explained. Eric St. Vincent Galt had a habit of abbreviating his middle name as St. V. and of forming his periods like small circles so that someone unacquainted with his name or his handwriting might read it as "Starvo."

There is the statement of a clerk at the Toronto Public Library who said he had helped a man answering Ray's description thread a microfilm viewing machine with microfilm copies of newspapers from 1932. Obviously Ray was looking at birth announcements, which gave birth date, father's name and mother's maiden name—the information necessary for obtaining duplicate birth certificates. He probably chose several names, looked them up in the Toronto telephone book, then hung around near their owners' homes hoping to get a glimpse of them, for he wanted to find men whose descriptions were similar to his own. Both Paul Edward Bridgman and Ramon George Sneyd remember receiving calls around the middle of April 1968 from a man who said he was with the Passport Division and wanted to know when they had last applied for a passport. Sneyd answered that he'd never had a passport. It was in the name Ramon George Sneyd that Ray applied for his. He used the Bridgman alias to rent his additional room in Toronto.

The Registrar of Births in Ottawa, Canada, produced two hand-printed, poorly spelled notes, mailed on different dates, requesting birth certificate copies for Paul Edward Bridgman and Ramon George Sneyd. All Ray needed to obtain these certificates was the information he'd obtained from the 1932 newspaper birth announcements. As to his passport, for which he applied as Ramon George Sneyd, the woman at the travel bureau in Toronto helped him fill out the necessary forms and make the formal application. Thanks to her help, he had to do little himself.

In short, say the Ray-alone people, if Ray had been part of a conspiracy the work of obtaining aliases, birth certificates, a passport, would have been done for him. He

James Earl Ray (right) and the three Toronto residents whose names he used as aliases before and after his alleged assassination of Martin Luther King, Jr. From left to right, Paul Bridgman, Eric St. Vincent Galt, and Ramon George Sneyd. (UNITED PRESS INTERNATIONAL TELEPHOTO)

would not have had to go to the public library, or send painstakingly hand-printed notes containing misspellings to the Registrar of Births, or seek the help of a travel agent in obtaining a passport, *or* wind up with a passport in the name of "Ramon George Sneya" instead of "Ramon George Sneyd." The whole operation, while clever, smacked of amateurism.

One of the conspiracy-backers' favorite aspects of the case is the possible "New Orleans connection." According to Ray, in December 1967, while he was in Los Angeles, he received a letter from Raoul telling him to drive to New Orleans on Friday December 15. Ray told Charlie Stein, whom he met in the downstairs bar of his hotel, about his intended trip and offered to take Stein with him. Ray told Stein he had business in New Orleans and was meeting friends he had known in Mexico. In New Orleans, according to Ray, he met Raoul and Raoul gave him $500 for expenses. Charlie Stein later testified that on the way down, Ray had stopped several times to make calls at service station telephone booths and that Ray had told him he had completed his business.

Neither Ray's first lawyer, Arthur Hanes, nor any of his subsequent lawyers has been successful in getting Ray to talk about New Orleans. Hanes says Ray seemed frightened of the city—indeed, of all Louisiana.

References to New Orleans had come up again and again in the Ray case. Four days after King's assassination, a black man named McFerren told the FBI about a conversation he had overheard in Memphis on the day of the assassination. He was shopping for produce in a wholesale establishment about 5 p.m. when he heard a man's voice in a small office near the loading dock. Glancing into the office, he saw two white men, one of whom was yelling into the telephone. "You're not going to get your pay until you do the job! . . . You can shoot [him] on the balcony!" The man banged down the receiver. Seconds later, the telephone rang again and the same man answered. "Don't come here," he shouted. "No, you can pick up the five thousand bucks from my brother in New Orleans."

On Wednesday April 10, six days after the assassination, a man calling himself Tony Benevitas visited a Memphis criminal attorney named Russell Thompson and informed him that his roommate had killed King. The roommate, whom he would call Pete, was still in Memphis. If he were caught, would Thompson defend him? Thompson never again heard from Benevitas, who said he came from *New Orleans.*

Lee Harvey Oswald, killer of President Kennedy, also

lived in New Orleans. Weren't there too many tie-ins with that city to be mere coincidence?

Those who believe Ray acted alone do not ascribe much validity to Ray's New Orleans activities and do not believe what little he has said about his trip to that city in December 1967. Ray said, for example, that he went to New Orleans in response to a letter he received from Raoul several days before the trip. At the time, Ray was seeing a psychiatrist. He saw him on Thursday, December 14 and made an appointment to see him again on Monday, December 18. But Friday morning he called to cancel the Monday appointment. Thursday night he had met Charlie Stein, who had asked him if he could drive to New Orleans the following morning, and he had agreed. Friday morning he also telephoned the National Dance Studio to say he would be out of town, which also indicates he did not decide to go to New Orleans until Thursday night.

Although the reports of McFerren and Benevitas have never been disproved, they do not seriously disturb those who believe that Ray acted alone. Benevitas was an admitted criminal and may simply have been one of the many crackpots or publicity- and attention-seekers who emerge after a major crime with stories that later prove false. McFerren may indeed have heard some sort of argument, but as happens with the most well-intentioned witnesses, he may not have remembered it correctly. After learning of King's assassination, his mind could have blended what he'd read and what he'd heard at the produce market and produced his "memory" of the mention of shooting someone on the balcony.

There are other points of contention. Why did Ray exchange the first gun he bought at the Aeromarine Supply Store? The conspiracy backers say he was told he had bought the wrong gun. The Ray-alone people say it was because he had discovered an imperfection in the first gun: a small metal burr in front of the chamber which prevented the bullet from slipping into it. Had Ray been familiar with guns, they say, he would simply have filed it down. But Ray was not accustomed to using such high-powered rifles, so he returned to the store, saying that his brother had told him it was the wrong gun, and exchanged the first gun for another.

How did Ray manage to get out of Memphis, considering that there were numerous alarms out for a white man in a white Mustang? The conspiracy backers insist that he must have been helped. The Ray-alone theorists point out that although such alarms were out, no all-points bulletins had been issued, no road blocks had been ordered set up, and other states had not been notified. They point to Ray's own explanation that he had simply gotten lost and had driven around side streets and back alleys while the police had naturally been watching the main highways.

The list of questions could fill a book. Even the most ardent Ray-alone theorists realize that certain questions have not as yet been answered satisfactorily. Still, they do not feel that these unanswered questions are sufficiently compelling to give credence to the conspiracy theory. The conspiracy backers think they do. Both sides are continually frustrated at being unable to present a theory with all the loose ends neatly tied up. Both sides are aware that they depend in part on the testimony of witnesses whose character is questionable at best. One of the chief prosecution witnesses in the Tennessee case against Ray was Charles Stephens, who was staying in Mrs. Brewer's rooming house in April 1968 and who identified Ray as the man he saw leaving the second floor bathroom with a gun immediately after the shooting. Yet, Stephens was a known drunkard. Both Robert Byron Watson and Clifford H. Andrews, whose reports of knowledge of a conspiracy have recently gained them renewed recognition, are convicted criminals. Even James Earl Ray's brother Jerry seems to have changed his statements. He told author George McMillan that the day after James's escape from prison Jerry, James, and Jack Ray met in a Chicago hotel, where James told his brothers he intended to kill King. Jerry also told McMillan, "The whole thing about Raoul and running drugs from Canada was bullshit. He went to Canada the first time to look the place over, to see how to get out of the country."

In January 1976, *Time* Magazine carried excerpts, including a report of this conversation, from McMillan's forthcoming book. The following month, *Time* carried a letter from Jerry Ray, which read in part:

> Does TIME think that George McMillan is smarter than the FBI? If not, then i would also be in Prison for helping in the King Murder. . . . You can beleive one thing, and that is if my brother James E. Ray committed the crime and did so without any help, then the Justice Department wouldnt be fighting so hard against him receiving a Trial.

Jerry Ray told McMillan that James telephoned him from Memphis on the morning of the murder and said he was going to get "the big nigger" that day. Now, Jerry Ray claims he did not talk to his brother on the day of the murder.

James Earl Ray himself has proved to be an unreliable witness who has changed parts of his story several times.

One change, that he was blocks away from Mrs. Brewer's rooming house when King was assassinated, interestingly was not made until after there had appeared in a Memphis newspaper the statement of an employee of a service station located some blocks from the rooming house that he had fixed a tire on a white Mustang some time before six o'clock on April 4, 1968.

Ray's supporters do not consider Ray's story changes damaging. "I don't think he's been inconsistent," said attorney Bernard Fensterwald in April 1976. "He's always maintained he was not at the scene of the crime. It's just that he's been asked so many detailed questions that unless he had a photographic memory, he's bound to have some discrepancies."

So the controversy continues, the Ray-alone people versus the conspiracy backers, the conspiracy backers against the Ray-alone people. Each group is a varied one, consisting of both people whose motives are suspect and people whose motives are above suspicion. The conspiracy group ranges from confirmed right-wingers to such respected newsmen as white reporter Jim Bishop, who wrote *The Days of Martin Luther King, Jr.*, and black *Chicago Daily News* reporter Carl T. Rowan. The Ray-alone group ranges from the FBI and the Justice Department, disclosures of whose illegal activities have cast suspicion on all of their activities, to respected authors who have spent months or years investigating the case, men like Gerold Frank and George McMillan. Each group comprises exploiters and men who have nothing to gain.

According to every poll taken, a majority of the American public favors the conspiracy theory, but this is more a statement of human psychology than of correct perception. We are shocked and dismayed when something like the assassination of a major leader occurs. How can we accept that a lone man is responsible? If we accept it, then we feel frightened, for how can a nation survive if its leaders are open every day to the bullets of mentally deranged assassins? It is easier to understand a plot, a step-by-step plan hatched in the netherworld that we know exists but that does not touch most of us. Since the disclosures of illegal intelligence activities, that netherworld has expanded beyond our ability to understand—frighteningly so, and we are suddenly prepared to believe anything.

Since the Watergate disclosures, the FBI and the CIA have been seen in a different light—not as our protectors but as our enemies, their legal and proper activities overshadowed by their illegal and improper ones. In the King case, perhaps the American public has overreacted to the disclosures of his harassment by the FBI. Beyond that, there has been no objective evidence, no proof, that the FBI was involved in the actual asssassination or engaged in any cover-up in the subsequent investigation. And yet those questions remain, and our desire for order, for neat and complete solutions, also remains. The situation is, as Norman Mailer has put it, like a jigsaw puzzle that is not yet complete but whose remaining pieces do not seem to fit together.

James Earl Ray is probably the only man alive who could fit together all the pieces in the jigsaw puzzle and point out which remaining pieces belong to some other set or belong nowhere at all. But James Earl Ray is not talking. He has been notably reticent about certain aspects of the case: what, if anything, happened in New Orleans, where he went and with whom, if anyone, he dealt between the time of the assassination and his capture in

London. Attorney Robert Livingston said of Ray in April 1976, "I think he's in some danger. He spoke up back in 1969, but they all chose to ignore him. Of course he isn't going around naming addresses and telephone numbers [of conspirators]. Let's just say he cares not to die."

Ray may be simply trying to maintain interest in the possibility of a conspiracy in order to further his case. Or, he may truly fear that if he talks he will be killed in prison. In the spring of 1976 one of his lawyers said his client had no interest in helping to "solve" the case, if indeed it had not already been solved. All Ray wanted was an acquittal. Was Ray part of a conspiracy? We may never know.

We will also never know how Martin Luther King, Jr., would have fared had he lived.

When Martin Luther King, Jr., was killed, the civil rights movement had effectively ended. Most of the legal bases for black equality in America had been laid. The cost had been great in human lives and property. But perhaps most costly of all, for black Americans, had been the loss of hope and faith in their fellow men and women. With the death of Martin Luther King, Jr., the resounding voice that had called for love and understanding between the races was stilled. It was replaced by young voices, like those of the Black Panthers, that cried for guns and guerrilla warfare in the city streets, that rejected all help from or trust of whites.

Martin Luther King, Jr., did not create the civil rights movement. He arose, at a critical time, to lead it. And although he was perhaps the most effective leader black America has ever known, he did not have—nor does any individual human being have—the ability to create a movement single-handedly.

Had he lived, it is likely that he would have maintained his position of leadership in any new movement that formed on the grass roots level against injustice or inequality. For it was at the forefront of such movements that Martin Luther King felt most alive and experienced his most inspired moments.

There would have been other moments for Martin Luther King, had he lived—some tragic and some joyous, some common to all men and some unique to a man in the public spotlight. He would have seen the illegal activities of his old nemesis, J. Edgar Hoover, and the FBI exposed, and he would have been subjected to a few uncomfortable public revelations about his private life. He would have suffered almost unbearable heartbreak over the senseless death of his mother, who was murdered by a deranged young black man during services at Ebenezer Baptist Church one Sunday in 1974. He would have watched with pride as his children grew up and his eldest son came to look remarkably like him. He would have watched and listened as his elderly father delivered one of the keynote speeches at the 1976 Democratic presidential convention, and been keenly aware of the implications of that event in our nation's bicentennial year. Had he lived . . .

That he did not is the fault not just of the man, or men, who killed him. Not letting up until the truth about his murder is told is important, but in our concern with the possibility of conspiracy, in our desire for neat solutions with no loose ends, we should not forget the climate of the times, and the mood of the people who set the tone of those times. In the broad sense, all of us, in a society that has not rid itself of bigotry, are responsible for the life, and the death, of Martin Luther King.

Selected Bibliography

American Daily Bulletin, January 2, 1976.

Bishop, Jim. *The Days of Martin Luther King, Jr.* New York: G. P. Putnam's Sons, 1971.

"Bus Boycott Anniversary," *Ebony,* February 1976.

Chicago *Daily News,* December 19, 1975.

"The Crusade to Topple King," *Time,* December 1, 1975.

Frank, Gerold. *An American Death.* Garden City, N.Y.: Doubleday & Co., Inc., 1972.

Haskins, James. *Profiles in Black Power.* Garden City, N.Y.: Doubleday & Co., Inc., 1972.

————. *Resistance: Profiles in Black Power.* Garden City, N.Y.: Doubleday & Co., 1970.

Huie, William Bradford. *He Slew the Dreamer.* New York: Delacorte Press, 1968.

Indianapolis *News,* 1975–1976.

Indianapolis *Recorder,* 1975–1976.

Indianapolis *Star,* 1975–1976.

"The King Assassination Revisited," *Time,* January 26, 1976.

"Letters," *Time,* February 16, 1976.

McMillan, George. *The Making of an Assassin*. Boston: Little, Brown & Co., 1976.

Murphy, Paul. "Don't Relax—They May Yet Be Alienable," *The National Observer*, November 22, 1975.

New York *Amsterdam News*, 1975–1976.

New York *Daily News*, 1975–1976.

New York *Post*, 1975–1976.

New York *Times*, 1975–1976.

"Nobody Asked: Is It Moral?" *Time*, May 10, 1976.

Reynolds, Barbara. "I Am Acting in the Name of Martin Luther King, Jr.," Chicago *Tribune* Magazine, January 11, 1976.

Rowan, Carl T. "Is There a Conspiracy Against Black Leaders?" *Ebony*, January 1976.

St. Louis Post-Dispatch, December 24, 1975.

"Tales of the FBI," *Newsweek*, December 1, 1975.

"The Truth About Hoover," *Time*, December 22, 1975.

Index